# Contents

*The real problem is not whether machines think but whether men do.*

−B.F. Skinner

# Acknowledgments

I would like to thank everyone who has made *HUMANLIKE* possible. Thank you to all the students and course participants who have shared with me your fascination and your concerns for all things AI, pushing me to dig deeper and look for answers.

I am grateful to my friends and colleagues who provided their generous feedback and invaluable insights. This book would not be the same without your support, thank you!

Thank you, Lucía and Alex, for being the bright lights in my life, reminding me what being human is all about. I love you.

I am especially grateful to Laura, my wife, not only has she encouraged me to share my views on AI with a wider audience, but she has taken the time to carefully read the book from cover to cover, offering invaluable advice. Thank you, Laura!

I am especially grateful to my wife, Laura, who, over the past two years, has encouraged me to share my views on AI with a wider audience. She has stood beside me through every late night and new idea, offering her unwavering support and insight. Not only did she believe in this vision, but she provided invaluable advice that strengthened this work in countless ways. With all my love and gratitude, thank you, Laura.

And thank you, the reader, for taking the time to explore these ideas with me.

# Why *HUMANLIKE*?
## AN INTRODUCTION

*Humanlike /ˈhjuːmənlaɪk/ ADJECTIVE entity, object, or behavior that shares certain attributes typically associated with humans, even if the entity is not human itself.*

When I saw the *I, Robot* movie in 2004 it never occurred to me that I was watching anything but sci-fi. Fast forward a few years and humanoid robots like the Atlas by Boston Dynamics blur the line between science fiction and science fact; not only can they navigate buildings with ease, but also perform highly acrobatic backflips (and dance!) much better than I ever could.

As I wrote *Disruption: Emerging Technologies and the Future of Work* in 2015 it did not seem possible for AI to write essays and poems, generate images, code in virtually any programming language and do everything else that generative AI (genAI) is capable of; I was convinced that creativity was off-limits for AI.

After tinkering furiously with ChatGPT for a month or so, it happened; I realized I was not dealing with a toy or niche technology. I got an intuition of genAI's transformative potential and while it's not human, it is eerily close: humanlike intelligence we can converse and create with.

11

So, I decided to discuss my findings with computer scientists, software engineers, business leaders, senior managers, Masters students, and anyone else who would listen. I noticed a pattern: participants' reactions spanned from fascination to terror (or both). More noticeably, some people would get emotional or even somewhat upset. At first, I didn't quite expect it or fully understand it, but then it hit me: we are interacting with a technology that can deal in arguably our two most precious currencies: intelligence and language, allowing it to produce outputs once exclusive to human minds. The thought that *something* could emulate such cherished capabilities, that define us as a species, was difficult to process.

All of this piqued my curiosity even further. But I had more questions than answers, on technical, business, and philosophical implications alike:

*How is it even possible to create AI systems that exhibit humanlike intelligence?*

*What is the likely impact of humanlike AI to enhance decision-making, drive innovation, and boost productivity while maintaining ethical standards?*

*What are the broader societal, ethical, and regulatory implications of AI systems that can think, learn, and adapt like humans?*

*What transformative role will humanlike AI play across industries, and how can individuals and organizations prepare for the evolving career landscapes?*

*Which skills might be valuable and in-demand in future job markets?*

*Etcetera...*

It was too late for me—I'd gone deep into the rabbit hole. I was determined to find the best available answers to satisfy my curiosity.

The book before you is the result of that continuing exploration: my attempt to make sense of the rapidly evolving AI landscape. The journey includes understanding what makes this type of AI humanlike as well as different from other types of software.

We will explore its applications but also limitations, along with risks and implementation challenges. The journey will include some thought experiments on the implications of increasing levels of autonomy for business and society at large.

Whether you're aiming to leverage AI for business, if you're a researcher or student, or if you are generally interested in the trajectory of artificial intelligence, especially generative AI, I hope that the insights gleaned here will give you a better intuition to make sense of increasingly humanlike AI and inform your decision-making.

## What you are about to read

In this book, we will discuss intelligence and how it has helped Homo sapiens secure the dominant position in the Planet. Then we will explore the decades-long quest to replicate intelligence and how we have arrived at humanlike capabilities. We will then define humanlike AI (hAI) as shorthand for the specific type of AI that can interact with us in a humanlike manner (including generative AI), regardless of its architecture. We will explore its current applications and industry use cases as well as its associated risks and challenges. We will then explore its trajectory and a roadmap toward human-level intelligence or Artificial General Intelligence as well as transformation scenarios and frameworks. We will close with a slightly more philosophical discussion of what it means to be human in the age of AI.

## Assumptions

This book sits at the intersection of business and artificial intelligence, yet it does *not* assume that the reader possesses any specialized knowledge. It is aimed at decision makers, students, and anyone with an interest in the trajectory and impact of humanlike AI... as you will see, there is an important role for all to play.

May you stay curious and enjoy the journey!

**Victor del Rosal**

1 October 2024

# 1

# Intelligence Built Civilization

## IT'S BEEN A GREAT QUARTER MILLION YEARS

*Man is a tool-using animal. Without tools he is nothing, with tools he is all.*

*—Thomas Carlyle*

The young hunter's heart pounds furiously as he sprints through the ancient pine forest chasing the wounded prey. His vision bounces with each stride, sweat trickling down his brow under the fading afternoon light. Ahead of him the wild boar remains just out of reach, barely managing to stay ahead. Two hunters trail closely, each wielding a hastily crafted wooden club. They've been chasing the animal for over an hour—pushing themselves to near exhaustion. The boar suddenly veers left and propels itself across a small stream into the dense thorny underbrush. The hunters plunge after it, but the creature is nowhere to be seen. Upset, they communicate with frantic grunts and wild gestures as they continue to search desperately... to no avail. It's gone. The precious sustenance—the third wild boar of the day—has slipped away. They will return empty-handed to their waiting tribe. The year is 80,000 Before Common Era (BCE).

## Forty thousand years later...

The hunters move in coordinated silence, sweeping through the thick Eurasian Forest as a unit, carrying spears expertly capped with beautiful yet deadly flint tips. Each spear shaft is adorned with carvings of delicate spirals and animal figures. Their target, a wild boar, has sensed their presence and is darting away from its human predators. The lead hunter catches the others' attention with a shift of his spear, a well-rehearsed command learned from childhood. Without hesitation the others drift sideways to block possible escape routes, guiding the boar into a narrowing ravine. They are moving swiftly without overexerting themselves. Their silent coordination is a stark contrast to the grunts and gestures of their ancestors. But none of this is accidental; their moves have been planned, the strategy now unfolding flawlessly. Near the end of the ravine, the boar seems close to an escape route, but in a split second, the ground suddenly gives way—the carefully interwoven branches camouflaged with leaves collapse under the weight of the boar, vanishing as if in slow motion into the void. It falls into a six-foot-deep hole—it's the end of its journey. Moments later, the hunters arrive, ready to bring back to the tribe their prized catch, their second of the day. What a difference 40 thousand years make.

## The transformation begins

Early humans became thinkers. Homo sapiens evolved from instinct-driven behaviors to more reflective thinking, strategic planning, and communication. Over

40 thousand years, they demonstrated newfound skills that enabled more efficient problem-solving and coordination, impacting daily life, social interactions and key activities such as hunting. Crucially, upgraded communication skills led to the development of language that enabled knowledge sharing—whatever they learned was not lost but could be passed down to the following generation. Humans could secure food and resources more reliably leading to better nutrition, improved living conditions, and overall, a higher quality of life. Artistic expressions, rituals and the use of symbols also marks this new cognitive era, fostering a shared sense of identity and belonging, shaping values and culture. These advancements reshaped their daily lives and set the stage for modern civilization. But what exactly happened to bring on the onset of this transformation? What triggered such changes?

## The Great Leap Forward

Our brains changed. It is believed that factors such as genetic mutations, changes in gene regulation and expression, changes in brain structure and plasticity, climate shifts, dietary improvements, environmental factors, increased social and cultural complexity, and sexual selection likely contributed to the evolution of the human brain. This mix of genetic, environmental, social, cultural, neurological, and evolutionary factors gradually improved brain functionalities, resulting in enhanced problem-solving, abstract thinking, and language capabilities. Symbolic thinking was a key aspect of this "upgrade", i.e., the ability to use symbols such as words, images, or objects to represent concepts, ideas, or other entities that are not physically present. This form of thought abstraction gave early Homo sapiens the ability to understand and communicate complex ideas, engage in creative expression, and create a knowledge base that would form the backbone driving innovation.

Arguably, the Great Leap Forward resulted in the improvement of the following cognitive abilities of early Homo sapiens:

| Cognitive Ability | Description |
|---|---|
| Memory | Improved capacity for both short-term and long-term memory, essential for knowledge retention and transmission. |
| Pattern Recognition | Enhanced ability to recognize patterns in the environment, important for survival and social interaction. |
| Emotional Regulation | The capacity to manage and regulate emotions, particularly in complex social situations, essential for maintaining social cohesion. |
| Problem-Solving | Enhanced ability to identify problems, devise solutions, and implement them effectively. |
| Abstract Thinking | The ability to think about objects, principles, and ideas that are not physically present. |
| Cognitive Flexibility | The ability to adapt thinking and behavior to changing circumstances, promoting resilience and problem-solving. |
| Symbolic Thinking | The ability to understand and create symbols, foundational for art, rituals, language, and culture. |
| Language and Communication | Development of complex language abilities, including grammar, syntax, and vocabulary, enabling precise and nuanced communication. |
| Planning and Foresight | The ability to anticipate future challenges and strategize solutions, crucial for survival and innovation. |
| Creativity and Imagination | The capacity for creative thinking and the imagination of new possibilities, leading to cultural and technological advancements. |
| Learning and Knowledge Transmission | The ability to learn from experience and others, and to pass on knowledge to subsequent generations, ensuring cultural continuity. |
| Self-Awareness and Metacognition | Improved self-awareness and the ability to reflect on one's thoughts, behaviors, and learning processes, crucial for personal development. |

*Figure 1. Mapping Cognitive Abilities*

While the causes are still up for debate, the effects were evident. Over roughly forty thousand years we became more intelligent. Human life became... better. Planning and foresight meant better access to food meaning we were able to feed ourselves better and lead healthier lives, increasing survival rates. Our brains were able to process increasingly complex social structures, paving the way for more efficient governance. Knowledge transmission allowed for the sharing and preservation of knowledge, allowing us to "stack" problem-solving know-how and tackle increasingly complex challenges. Complex language led to the emergence of culture incorporating art, religion, rituals, etc. fostering a sense of identity and continuity.

An overview of the likely impacts of cognitive improvements can be summarized as follows:

| Area of Impact | Description |
|---|---|
| Health and Survival | Improved problem-solving and adaptability enhanced humans' ability to manage resources, develop agriculture, and innovate in healthcare practices, directly impacting survival and health. |
| Environment and Resource Management | Advanced planning and foresight enabled humans to manage and manipulate their environment more effectively, leading to agricultural development, settlement formation, and resource sustainability. |
| Social Structures | Enhanced communication, emotional regulation, and cooperation enabled the formation of larger, more complex social structures, including hierarchical societies and governance systems. |
| Education and Knowledge Transmission | Enhanced memory and communication skills allowed for the accumulation and sharing of knowledge across generations, leading to the development of formal education systems and the preservation of cultural and technological knowledge. |
| Technology and Innovation | Advanced problem-solving, planning, and cognitive flexibility led to the creation of sophisticated tools, technologies, and long-term projects, driving human progress. |
| Exploration and Migration | Enhanced planning, problem-solving, and pattern recognition abilities enabled long-distance exploration, navigation, and the colonization of diverse environments, supporting global human expansion. |
| Culture | The development of complex language, symbolic thinking, and creativity led to the emergence of art, religion, rituals, myths, and shared narratives, fostering cultural identity and continuity. |
| Adaptability | Cognitive flexibility and problem-solving abilities allowed cultures to adapt to environmental changes, technological shifts, and social challenges, ensuring long-term resilience and survival. |

*Figure 2. Speculative Impacts of Cognitive Improvements in Early Homo sapiens*

All in all, this brain "upgrade" some 50 thousand years ago laid the foundation of modern civilization, helping humans lead safer, richer, more productive lives.

Intelligence has been the crucial catalyst for human progress, enabling all sorts of human progress. As a side note, we must be thankful to live on a planet with a relatively stable climate for the past quarter million years. We agree that human intelligence has played a key role in driving civilization forward over the millennia, with the compounding effects of knowledge sharing. So, it might be useful to take a closer look at intelligence. The full range of cognitive abilities that we call intelligence is the primary enabler of human progress.

## Defining intelligence

Surprisingly, there isn't a single universally accepted definition of intelligence.

David Wechsler, known for developing the Wechsler Adult Intelligence Scale (WAIS), defines it as "the aggregate or global capacity of the individual to act purposefully, to think rationally, and to deal effectively with the environment." He viewed intelligence as a multifaceted construct that encompasses various cognitive abilities, including verbal comprehension, perceptual reasoning, working memory, and processing speed, all contributing to an individual's overall adaptability.

Howard Gardner, best known for his theory of Multiple Intelligences, defines it as "the ability to solve problems, or to create products, that are valued within one or more cultural settings." He challenges the traditional notion of a single, general intelligence, proposing instead that there are several distinct forms of intelligence, such as linguistic, logical-mathematical, spatial, and interpersonal, each important in different contexts. Gardner also discusses that intelligence involves a person's ability to understand and interact effectively with their surroundings.

Jean Piaget, a pioneer in the study of child development, defines intelligence as "the ability to adapt to one's environment, to learn from experience, and to apply knowledge to new situations." Piaget believed that intelligence is a dynamic process that develops through stages, starting with basic sensorimotor abilities, progressing to more complex abstract thinking, reflecting an individual's capacity to adapt and solve problems in a changing world.

A systems theory view would break it down into three key elements: inputs, process, and outputs, whereby the processor, i.e., the brain, learns and becomes more effective at producing outputs aligned with certain goals.

Researcher Linda Gottfredson's definition is quoted across a number of scientific journals, describing intelligence as "a very general mental capability that, among other things, involves the ability to reason, plan, solve problems, think abstractly, comprehend complex ideas, learn quickly, and learn from experience." This broader perspective encompasses theoretical and practical elements.

This multifaceted definition emphasizes that intelligence is not a single trait but a complex interplay of various cognitive abilities that enable individuals to interact with their environment. Let us approximate our definition of intelligence thus far:

*Intelligence is the cognitive ability to acquire, process, and apply knowledge and skills across diverse situations. It involves learning from experience, adapting to new environments, reasoning logically, solving problems, thinking abstractly, and achieving goals. This multifaceted capacity empowers individuals to navigate challenges, come up with solutions, and engage meaningfully with their environment.*

As we transition in the following chapters toward defining intelligence in the context of artificial intelligence, it will be useful to introduce the following concept:

## Agent

An agent is an entity that perceives its environment through sensors, processes information, and acts upon that environment through actuators to achieve specific goals or objectives.

It could be argued that an agent, whether human or not, is said to be intelligent if it can process information and adapt to environmental challenges; if it can reason logically, and solve problems; if it can learn from experience and apply knowledge to novel situations; if it can understand complex ideas and engage in purposeful action; and if it has the potential to create valuable outputs.

## Language as an Expression of Intelligence

As seen, defining intelligence is not a straightforward process. So, it might be useful to find a proxy for it. Could language be both an expression and a significant indicator of human intelligence?

Language reflects the advanced cognitive processes that distinguish us from other species. The evolution from simple gestures and vocalizations to sophisticated language—with grammar, syntax, and an extensive vocabulary—marks a significant leap in neural development. This progression enabled our ancestors not only to communicate immediate needs but also to convey abstract concepts, share intricate ideas, and plan for the future. The emergence of language facilitated effective knowledge transmission, allowing information to be preserved and built upon across generations.

The complexity of human language requires intricate neural processing. Specific regions of the brain linked to language comprehension highlight the dedicated neural architecture that supports our linguistic abilities. Linguist Noam Chomsky proposed the theory of an innate "language acquisition device," suggesting that humans are uniquely equipped with a neurological foundation for language learning, underscoring the specialized evolution of our brains.

Language is not merely a tool for communication; it reflects advanced cognitive functions such as abstract thinking, problem-solving, and self-awareness. It enables us to engage in symbolic thinking—the ability to understand and manipulate symbols—which is fundamental to art, science, and culture. Lev Vygotsky emphasized that language is crucial for cognitive development, serving as the primary means through which we internalize complex concepts and cultural norms.

Language represents a remarkable achievement of human cognition, allowing us to communicate complex ideas, abstract concepts, and subtle emotions with incredible nuance and precision. Moreover, could it be an indicator of intelligence? Can language serve as a proxy for cognitive complexity? Let's consider some aspects pointing to this:

## Language as a Proxy of Cognitive Complexity

The structure of human language reveals the remarkable complexity of our minds in several key ways. First, consider how we build meaning: we can combine simple ideas to create complex ones, nest thoughts within thoughts, and create layers of meaning that go far beyond basic communication. Look at how we handle grammar—we can effortlessly use different tenses, moods, and complex sentence structures. When we say something like "If I had known about the traffic, I would have left earlier," we're actually doing several sophisticated things at once: imagining different scenarios, understanding time, applying grammar rules, and connecting causes with effects.

But language does much more than just combine ideas. It lets us work with abstract concepts that have no physical form—we can discuss ideas like "justice," "tomorrow," or "possibility" just as easily as we talk about trees or stones. We can share not just what we see and feel right now, but also our hopes, fears, and imaginings about the future. This ability to work with abstract ideas through language points to advanced mental capabilities like reasoning, planning, and problem-solving. We even create new words when we need them, showing how language enables creativity and innovation in thinking.

Our brains are doing remarkable juggling acts when we use language. We're constantly paying attention to what we want to say while filtering out what we shouldn't say, adapting our words to fit different social situations, and even switching between languages if we speak more than one. People who speak multiple languages show us just how flexible our minds can be— they switch between completely different language systems seamlessly, often without even thinking about it.

Perhaps even more fascinating is how we adjust our language based on who we're talking to. When we say "it's cold in here," we might actually mean "please close the window," and our listeners usually understand this perfectly. This shows how our brains seamlessly combine language with social understanding. We constantly consider what others know and believe, adjusting our words to fit the situation—a skill psychologists call "theory of mind," which reveals sophisticated social thinking.

Our relationship with language goes even deeper. We can think and talk about language itself—analyzing its patterns, learning new languages, and understanding metaphors. This ability to step back and examine our own tools of thought shows a remarkable level of mental sophistication. Scientists studying the brain have found that when we use language, we're activating multiple connected regions, each handling different aspects of meaning, memory, and social understanding. It's like having an orchestra in our heads, with different sections working together to create something complex and beautiful.

Watch how a child learns language, and you'll see a mirror of how human thinking develops. They start with simple words and gradually master complex grammar, abstract concepts, and social rules. This journey from basic communication to sophisticated language use shows us how closely language and thinking are connected. As children's minds develop, their language becomes more complex—they learn to tell stories, understand jokes, and grasp subtle meanings.

Language also serves as our primary tool for passing knowledge from one generation to the next. Through stories, explanations, and teachings, we build upon the wisdom of those who came before us. This ability to accumulate and transmit knowledge through language has been crucial for human progress, allowing each generation to start where the previous one left off. The way we use language to organize and store information—through narratives, categories, and patterns—helps us remember and understand our world better.

Looking at all these aspects of language—from its intricate structure to its role in memory and learning, from its social nature to its power in sharing knowledge—we can see why it serves as such a good indicator of cognitive complexity. Language isn't just a tool for communication; it's a window into the sophisticated mental capabilities that make us human. It shows us how we think, how we understand others, and how we make sense of our world.

We will assume that this general-purpose collection of cognitive capabilities we refer to as intelligence is a highly valuable resource and that language is a key expression of it.

Later in the book we will address the brain's own complexity. But for now, let's say that we wanted to replicate cognitive capabilities through artificial means. How could that be possibly achieved... or even attempted?

# 2

## Thinking Machines
EMULATING INTELLIGENCE

*Man must rise above the Earth—to the top of the atmosphere and beyond—for only thus will he fully understand the world in which he lives.*

*—Socrates*

To prepare for space exploration, Neil Armstrong test-piloted the rocket-powered North American X-15 aircraft seven times between 1960 and 1962. The X-15 would be mounted under the wing of a B-52 Stratofortress and then released at around 45,000 feet, at which point it would switch on its XLR99 rocket engine roughly generating the combined thrust of two Boeing 737 jet engines. During his flights, Armstrong reached a peak speed of 4,370 mph (7,040 km/h, Mach 5.74) and a maximum altitude of 207,500 feet, about six times the cruising altitude of a commercial airliner. In 1967, William J. "Pete" Knight set a record speed of 4,520 mph (7,274 km/h, Mach 6.7) making the X-15 the fastest manned aircraft ever flown. Another significant milestone achieved on the aircraft took place in 1963, when Joseph A. Walker surpassed the Kármán line, the official boundary of space at 100 kilometers from Earth's surface, climbing to an altitude of 354,200 feet (62 miles, 108 kilometers). These achievements might not seem extraordinary today except for the fact that, barely sixty years before that, humanity had not even taken to the skies.

## The Wright Flyer I

Now picture the Wright Flyer I, the aircraft built by the Wright brothers, which was the first to achieve powered, controlled, and sustained flight. Its maiden voyage on December 17, 1903, lasted just 12 seconds and reached an airspeed of about 31 mph (50 km/h) while covering a distance of 120 feet (37 meters)—only a third of the length of a soccer field. It was powered by a custom-built 12-horsepower engine driving two propellers; in comparison, the typical car today generates ten to twenty times more horsepower.

As modest as it was, this event ushered in the era of aviation at a time of skepticism toward the possibility of human flight. In the late 1800s and early 1900s, the prevalent belief was that heavier-than-air flight was impossible. Yet, in just six decades we went from barely being able to take off the ground to flying into space; the quest to build flying machines not only materialized but has grown steadily becoming the key industry that it is today. However, for centuries, it remained an elusive dream.

## The Dream of Flight

The earliest references to human flight are documented in Greek mythology. One famous myth tells of Daedalus, a talented craftsman who created wings for himself and his son, Icarus, to escape imprisonment on the island of Crete. Ignoring his father's warning, Icarus flew too close to the sun and fell to his death when his wings melted. The story, while tragic, symbolizes both the ambition and the danger associated with the dream of flight.

One of the first documented flying machine blueprints comes from the Renaissance, when Leonardo da Vinci designed the ornithopter to mimic the flapping motion of a bird's wings. However, it was not built during his lifetime and likely would not have been successful.

The 18th and 19th centuries brought a more scientific approach. Sir George Cayley, often called the "father of modern aeronautics," laid the foundation for the modern airplane identifying the four forces involved in flight: lift, weight, thrust, and drag; he built the first successful human-carrying glider in the early 1800s. Crucially, his work shifted the focus from mimicking bird flight to understanding aerodynamic principles. This was a key departure from an architectural approach to a functional one, i.e., instead of aiming to recreate the *process* by which a bird flies—by flapping wings— focusing on the *outcome*—flying—underpinned by first-principles thinking.

The late 19th century saw numerous attempts to achieve powered flight including inventors such as Otto Lilienthal testing gliders and providing critical data on aerodynamics. Despite the skepticism, the public remained fascinated by the possibility of flight. The failures of early flying machines often led to ridicule, yet they also stoked curiosity and hope. One inventor that came extremely close was Samuel Pierpont Langley, who like the Wright brothers experimented with powered models. Also in December 1903, his *Aerodrome A* briefly lifted off the air but did not achieve sustained, controlled flight. This persistence and steady scientific progress kept the dream alive, culminating on that fateful December 17, 1903, when humans finally took to the skies, albeit briefly, rewarding centuries of dreams and effort.

However, the inspiration for flight came from birds (or as we might playfully call them, the OGs—Original Gliders), i.e., the organic systems that inspired flying machines. And while human ingenuity has managed to dramatically surpass them in speed, altitude, and range, for millennia birds were the only show in town, rulers of the skies. Yet a functionality exclusive to an organic life form was successfully emulated through artificial means.

Could the same thing be happening to intelligence?

As we will see, the imitation journey of flight offers a powerful analogy for humanity's dream to artificially emulate intelligence.

## The Quest to Build Thinking Machines

After setting out to define intelligence we wondered if it could be replicated. Now, imagine that *you* are given the (daunting) challenge of creating a system that is truly intelligent. Gulp. Is it possible to build a thinking machine? Let's find out. But first let's look at a few questions that you might have:

What could be a good starting point to approach the task of emulating intelligence?

Would you focus on logic and rules, perhaps approaching it like a vast decision tree, mapping out all possible outcomes?

Would you aim to mimic how humans learn and adapt through trial and error?

How could creativity—essential to problem-solving—be emulated?

How would you ensure that the intelligence you're emulating can generalize knowledge across different domains?

Etcetera...

It is no simple task, so let's explore how this challenge has been approached so far.

## Emulation

"The process of copying something achieved by someone else and trying to do it as well as they have."

—Cambridge University Press. (2024). Emulation. Cambridge Advanced Learner's Dictionary & Thesaurus.

Emulation is the act of copying or imitating the characteristics, behavior, or performance of one entity by another. Emulation involves striving to match or surpass the qualities or achievements of a model, whether it's a person, a process, or a system, by closely replicating or adapting the methods, styles, or techniques used by the original.

The earliest attempts to emulate intelligence can be traced back to the 4th to 5th centuries BCE. Ancient Greek mythology often featured automata—beings with humanlike intelligence such as Talos, a giant bronze automaton, reflected early human curiosity about artificial beings with humanlike qualities.

Around the 4th century BCE, Aristotle's work on syllogistic reasoning, a form of reasoning connecting two premises, became a precursor to formal logic. He demonstrated how a logical conclusion could be derived from a general premise, for example, in the syllogism "if A is B and B is C, then A is C." This method of reasoning would later become a foundational element in computer science.

During the Middle Ages and the Renaissance, inventors such as Al-Jazari and Leonardo da Vinci created mechanical automata, self-operating machines such as water clocks and robotic knights designed to mimic human or animal actions. As simple as they were, they demonstrated an early interest in replicating aspects of human or animal behavior.

In the 17th century, Descartes' proposed the concept of dualism, a philosophical view positing that mind and body are fundamentally separate entities. It opened the possibility that mental processes, such as logical reasoning, perception, and self-awareness, could potentially exist outside the biological brain. Given that mind and body were previously seen as a unit, dualism inspired inventors to create thinking machines.

The 18th century further advanced this with the creation of more sophisticated mechanical figures, such as Jacques de Vaucanson's flute player and The Digesting Duck, which could perform complex tasks. Although not intelligent by any modern definition, these devices were remarkable feats of engineering that imitated certain life processes.

In the 19th century, the formalization of logic and mathematics became central to the future development of artificial intelligence. George Boole's development of Boolean algebra allowed logical statements to be expressed mathematically, laying a foundation for computational logic. Simultaneously, Charles Babbage, often called the "father of the computer," designed the Analytical Engine as a general-purpose machine capable of performing any mathematical calculation that used gears and levers and looked like a large mechanical loom. Ada Lovelace envisioned its potential beyond mere calculation, foreseeing the possibility of a machine capable of processing information in humanlike ways. She also described how the machine could be programmed to execute a series of operations, laying the groundwork for the field of programming.

Alan Turing's concept of the Turing Machine, introduced in 1936, was pivotal in shaping the theoretical framework of computing. A Turing machine is a computational model consisting of a hypothetically infinite tape divided into cells, where each cell can hold a symbol (typically 0 or 1), a read/write head that can move along the tape, a state register that holds the current state of the machine, and a set of rules (a program) that directs the machine's actions based on the current state and the symbol being read. It is significant because it defines what it means for a function to be computable, i.e., it helps determine if a problem can be solved by an algorithm. Given that a Turing Machine is designed to perform one specific computation, you would need a separate Turing Machine designed specifically to solve each type of problem. That's where the Universal Turing Machine (UTM) comes in. It is a special type of Turing Machine that can simulate any other Turing Machine, taking its description and simulating its behavior, becoming a general-purpose machine.

Following Turing's seminal work, several key computing devices were built, starting with the Zuse Z3 in 1941, the world's first programmable digital computer using binary system computation, developed by Konrad Zuse in Germany. In 1944, Howard Aiken and IBM created the Harvard Mark I, an electromechanical machine combining mechanical and electrical components. The Electronic Numerical Integrator and Computer (ENIAC), completed in 1945, was the first fully electronic general-purpose digital computer, using vacuum tubes for vastly improved speed and versatility. Building on this, the Electronic Discrete Variable Automatic Computer (EDVAC) introduced the stored-program concept, influenced by

Turing's Universal Machine. These pioneering mechanical and electrical computers laid the groundwork for modern computing and AI.

In the journey to emulate intelligence, ideas and practice slowly intertwined, stacking the necessary theoretical and technical foundations toward the goal of building thinking machines. From mythology and simple automata to gear-based and more modern electrical machines, each phase—whether philosophical, theoretical, computational, or mechanical—becomes the starting point for the next one, getting us closer to answering the question: is it even possible to emulate human intelligence—can we build thinking machines?

# 3
# Artificial Intelligence
## A BRIEF HISTORY

*The most profound technologies are those that disappear.*
*They weave themselves into the fabric of everyday life until*
*they are indistinguishable from it.*

*—Mark Weiser*

Following the foundational developments in computing and logic, the quest to build thinking machines gained momentum in the mid-20th century. From June 18 to August 17, 1956, researchers including John McCarthy, Marvin Minsky, Nathaniel Rochester, and Claude Shannon gathered at the Dartmouth Conference, aiming to make machines that could "think" like humans. They proposed that "every aspect of learning or any other feature of intelligence can in principle be so precisely described that a machine can be made to simulate it." John McCarthy is credited with coining the term "Artificial Intelligence" as part of the conference proposal, marking the formal beginning of AI as a field of study.

## The Early Approaches: Symbolic AI and Logic-Based Systems

The initial phase of AI research was dominated by symbolic AI, also known as "Good Old-Fashioned AI" (GOFAI). This approach involved encoding human knowledge and reasoning processes into computers using symbols and logical rules. The idea was to create systems that could perform tasks traditionally requiring human intelligence, such as playing chess or solving mathematical theorems. Early successes included programs like the Logic Theorist and the General Problem Solver, which demonstrated the potential of AI in solving complex problems.

However, symbolic AI had its limitations. While it excelled at solving well-defined problems with clear rules, it struggled with tasks that required perception, learning from experience, or dealing with the ambiguity of the real world. The brittleness of these systems, meaning their inability to handle unforeseen situations, became a significant challenge.

## The Rise of Connectionism: Artificial Neural Networks

In response to the limitations of symbolic AI, a different approach emerged in the form of connectionism, which focused on creating systems that could learn and adapt rather than relying solely on predefined rules. This approach was inspired by the structure of the human brain, particularly the networks of neurons that process and transmit information.

Artificial Neural Networks (ANNs) were developed to mimic these biological processes, allowing machines to learn from data through a process of adjusting the connections between artificial neurons. Early work by researchers like Frank Rosenblatt, who developed the

Perceptron in 1958, laid the groundwork for what would later become a central pillar of AI research.

However, the progress of ANNs was slow due to the limitations of computing power and the lack of large datasets. By the 1970s, AI research experienced a period known as the "AI winter," marked by reduced funding and interest due to unmet expectations.

## Expert Systems and Knowledge-Based AI

In the 1980s, AI experienced a resurgence with the development of expert systems—programs designed to emulate the decision-making ability of a human expert in specific domains. These systems, such as MYCIN for medical diagnosis and DENDRAL for chemical analysis, used vast databases of knowledge and inference rules to provide expert-level advice.

Expert systems were widely adopted in industries ranging from finance to healthcare, demonstrating the practical applications of AI. However, like symbolic AI, they were limited by their reliance on explicit knowledge and rules, making them rigid and difficult to scale.

## The Deep Learning Revolution

Advances in computing power, the availability of massive datasets, and breakthroughs in machine learning techniques ushered in a new era for AI. The re-emergence of deep learning, a subfield of machine learning based on multi-layered artificial neural networks, revolutionized the field.

Deep learning models, such as convolutional neural networks (CNNs) and recurrent neural networks (RNNs), excelled at tasks involving image and speech recognition, natural language processing, and game playing. Landmark achievements, such as Google's AlphaGo defeating a world champion Go player and the rise of virtual assistants like Siri and Alexa, showcased the potential of AI to tackle complex, real-world problems.

## Deep Learning

Deep learning is a subfield of machine learning that leverages neural networks with multiple layers, often referred to as "deep" networks, to model intricate patterns and representations in large datasets. Unlike traditional machine learning, where features are often manually extracted, deep learning models automatically discover relevant features during training. This is achieved by processing data through several hidden layers, where each layer captures increasingly abstract and complex features of the input. The depth and complexity of these networks allow deep learning models to excel in tasks such as image recognition, natural language processing, and game playing by effectively learning from vast amounts of data and generalizing from it.

However, the true power of deep learning lies in its ability to extract and represent complex patterns from vast amounts of data, a capability that has been enhanced by the development of more sophisticated architectures like Transformers, which have transformed natural language processing, enabling models like GPT-3 and its successors to generate humanlike text. These advancements have expanded the horizons of AI, allowing it to perform tasks that were once considered the exclusive domain of human intelligence.

## Modern AI: Hybrid Approaches and the Future

Today, AI research is marked by a convergence of approaches, combining symbolic AI, connectionism, and new paradigms like reinforcement learning, where systems learn to make decisions through trial and error in dynamic environments. Hybrid systems that integrate symbolic reasoning with deep learning are also gaining traction, aiming to combine the strengths of both approaches.

Deep learning continues to evolve, with innovations such as unsupervised learning, self-supervised learning, and transfer learning pushing the boundaries of what AI systems can achieve. These techniques allow models to learn with less human intervention, adapt to new tasks with minimal data, and generalize knowledge across different domains, bringing us closer to the goal of building general humanlike intelligence, that is, Artificial General Intelligence (AGI).

## The Quest to Build Thinking Machines

To recap, the challenge of building thinking machines was approached by first trying to replicate human reasoning using symbolic AI, which involved programming computers with rules and logic to solve specific problems. However, this method struggled with tasks that required flexibility or learning from experience. To overcome these limitations, researchers developed artificial neural networks, inspired by the human brain, allowing machines to learn and adapt through data. Over time, with advances in computing power and techniques like deep learning, which uses layered neural networks to recognize patterns in vast amounts of data, AI became more capable of handling complex tasks like understanding language or recognizing images. Today, AI research combines different methods—rules-based logic, learning from data, and trial-and-error learning—to create systems that can think and adapt more like humans, bringing us closer to the dream of truly intelligent machines.

## Neural Networks and Deep Learning

Traditional AI methods, such as symbolic AI, worked well in closed domains such as chess or algebra as they relied heavily on explicit programming and predefined rules to solve problems. However, they could easily be thrown off in open-ended domains such as language, where words can have multiple possible interpretations.

Neural networks, on the other hand, introduced a new approach where machines could learn patterns and make decisions by processing data through interconnected layers of artificial neurons, in a manner inspired by the human brain's learning process. This shift enabled AI systems to tackle more complex and less structured tasks, including image recognition and language translation, previously beyond reach.

Deep neural networks allowed machines to automatically learn from raw data. The depth of these networks empowered them to excel at tasks involving massive amounts of data, such as speech recognition and image classification. They even began outperforming humans in games that were considered intractable such as the millenary game of Go, as demonstrated by AlphaGo's success in strategic gameplay. Neural networks and deep learning have led to breakthroughs across diverse domains, making AI more of a natural learner, able to make better sense of data.

## Neural networks

Neural networks are computational models inspired by the structure and functioning of the human brain. They consist of layers of interconnected nodes, or "neurons," where each connection carries a weight that adjusts as learning occurs. Information is passed through the network, with each neuron applying a function to its inputs and passing the result to the next layer. This process allows the network to learn complex patterns in data by adjusting the weights through a process called backpropagation, where errors are calculated and used to fine-tune the network's parameters. Over time, neural networks can make predictions, classify data, or generate new information by recognizing patterns and relationships within the data they have been trained on.

**Getting closer to building thinking machines**

As researchers continue to push the boundaries of what machines can achieve, the dream of building thinking machines moves closer to reality.

Just like aviation went from the Wright Flyer I to the X-15 over six decades, AI has evolved from simple rule-based systems to advanced, adaptive technologies, moving closer to achieving true machine intelligence and revolutionizing how we interact with the world.

Sixty-six years passed between the launch of AI as a formal field and another significant milestone: the dawn of the generative AI era, the day when ChatGPT went mainstream on November 30, 2022.

But what exactly is generative AI and why is it a significant evolution in the quest to replicate human intelligence?

## A Unified Definition of Intelligence

First, let's revisit our definition of intelligence, this time with the vantage point of computer science. Stuart Russell and Peter Norvig, co-authors of the *Artificial Intelligence: A Modern Approach* textbook do not explicitly define intelligence but refer to it as the ability (of an agent) to achieve goals or solve problems in an optimal or near-optimal way, given a set of constraints and the available information. In essence, they see intelligence as the capacity to act rationally, where rationality is defined as making decisions that are expected to achieve specific objectives effectively and efficiently.

Prominent AI researchers Shane Legg and Marcus Hutter define intelligence in their 2007 paper *Universal Intelligence: A Definition of Machine Intelligence* as follows:

"Intelligence measures an agent's ability to achieve goals in a wide range of environments."

## Proposing a Definition of Intelligence

The nature of intelligence is still debated: is it a single general ability or composed of multiple specialized abilities? How can it be accurately measured? The functional definition of intelligence by Legg & Hutter has proven useful in guiding the field's efforts, as it is pragmatic, focused on outputs, i.e., goal achievement:

*Intelligence measures an agent's ability to achieve goals in a wide range of environments*

However, a more complete and nuanced definition that incorporates classical definitions will be more useful for our purposes:

## Intelligence

Intelligence is the adaptive capacity to pursue goals effectively across diverse environments, characterized by the ability to process information, acquire knowledge, reason logically, and solve problems. It involves learning from experience, applying insights to new situations, engaging in abstract thinking, and generating creative ideas. Additionally, intelligence can encompass strategic planning, and the ability to navigate challenges and generate solutions. It can be measured by an agent's ability to optimally achieve objectives within various constraints and scenarios. It is a dynamic, multifaceted capability drawing from, but not limited to spatial awareness, social understanding, and emotional perception.

# 4
## Growing a Brain
### HUMANLIKE INTELLIGENCE

*The mind is not a vessel to be filled, but a fire to be kindled.*

*–Plutarch*

Y*ou wake up in the middle of the night, startled, thinking you must have had a nightmare. But you're not at home. The gentle rocking and the waves crashing against your light vessel remind you that you are in deep sea. But something is off. You head to the bridge to check your instruments, and you're immediately alarmed. This can't be. The biodiversity research vessel you captain,* The Curiosity, *which departed from Sydney some eleven days ago is supposed to be midway through its 3,675 nautical mile journey headed to the Easter Islands. However, you are inexplicably off course. More importantly you cannot hear the light hum of the engines.*

*"This can't be," you mutter in disbelief.*

*You check your position to find that, ironically, you've drifted near Point Nemo, the most remote point on Earth, where sometimes the nearest humans are the astronauts on board the International Space Station.*

*Suddenly, you are reminded of Captain Nemo, the anti-hero from Jules Verne's 20,000 Leagues Under the Sea. Alex, your expedition leader, confirms your location. Now the spine-tingling loneliness sinks in, it embraces you, meeting you in the middle of nowhere.*

*You make a mental note to keep calm and then take two deep breaths*

*Someone from your crew breaks the silence:*

*"What do we do now, Captain?"*

Let's try to understand what has just happened in your brain as you read the story.

## Brain architecture

At its core, the human brain can be understood as a network of specialized regions that work together to process information, control bodily functions, and facilitate thought, emotion, and behavior. It is composed of three main parts: the cerebrum, the cerebellum, and the brainstem. The cerebrum, the largest part, is responsible for higher cognitive functions like thinking, decision-making, and emotions. It is divided into two hemispheres, each controlling opposite sides of the body, and further into four lobes: the frontal (decision-making and movement), parietal (sensory processing), temporal (hearing and memory), and occipital (vision). Below the cerebrum, the cerebellum coordinates muscle movements and maintains balance and posture. The brainstem, connecting the brain to the spinal cord, controls vital involuntary functions like breathing, heart rate, and sleep. From a vast network of approximately 86 billion interconnected neurons, our memories are stored, our thoughts take shape, and our personalities emerge, and we can function as human beings.

## *Curiosity* from the Brain's Point of View

When reading the story of yourself as the captain of *Curiosity*, your brain embarks on a complex journey of sensory processing, language comprehension, and memory retrieval. As your eyes scan the words, your visual cortex decodes the text into familiar symbols, while your brain's language centers in the frontal and temporal lobes work together to understand and mentally vocalize the narrative. This allows you to not just read, but to experience the story, as though you're hearing the words in your mind.

Simultaneously, your parietal lobe helps you visualize the scene, mapping the vast ocean, the inky blue waters, and the tension aboard the ship. Your hippocampus and neocortex tap into long-term memories, allowing you to connect the unfolding tale with prior knowledge—whether it's your familiarity with Jules Verne's *Twenty Thousand Leagues Under the Sea*, the geographical isolation of Point Nemo, or even your own experiences of uncertainty and responsibility.

As your brain integrates these sensory inputs and memories, your cerebellum subtly adjusts your posture and physical responses, perhaps causing you to tense or lean forward as the narrative's tension builds. This interplay of neural processes creates a vivid mental world where you, as the captain, navigate both the literal and figurative currents of the story.

The frontal lobe engages in decision-making, helping you empathize with the captain's challenges, while the occipital lobe translates the written words into the vivid images that unfold in your mind. This intricate coordination between the brain's regions—sensory decoding in the visual cortex, language comprehension in the frontal and temporal lobes, visualization by the parietal lobe, and physical response managed by the cerebellum—allows you to fully immerse yourself in the narrative, making it a deeply personal and engaging experience

Trying to replicate *all* that the brain does is indeed a daunting proposition. But let's be reminded of our birds-to-airplane analogy: we are not trying to replicate the full brain *architecture*—how exactly it works—but instead its *functionality*—what it can do. To make it simpler, let's focus on one aspect of intelligence: language. As previously discussed, language is an expression of intelligence and a key indicator of it. Would it be possible to grow a *synthetic* brain that can understand and process language? Could this get us closer to emulating intelligence?

## The Transformer Architecture

Before 2017, AI models had limitations, especially when it came to processing long pieces of information.

They worked step-by-step, which made them slow and often missed the true meaning in a string of text, particularly when understanding context was crucial. This is where the Transformer architecture came in and transformed the game.

The breakthrough came from Google researchers in a 2017 paper called "Attention is All You Need." They introduced a new AI model—the Transformer—that fundamentally changed how AI handles data, particularly language. This model became the foundation for modern generative AI systems, which can produce text, images, code, and much more.

At its core, the Transformer is designed to process information all at once, instead of step-by-step. It can look at the relationships between different parts of a sentence or data sequence simultaneously, which makes it faster and better at understanding context. For example, it can figure out which words in a sentence are most important in relation to others, helping the AI grasp meaning much more accurately.

To take this a step further, the Transformer uses multiple attention mechanisms—called "multi-head attention." This allows it to focus on different aspects of the data at the same time. It is like having several sets of eyes, each looking at the same information from a different angle. For instance, when analyzing a sentence, one "head" might focus on the action while another might focus on the time or setting.

Additionally, the model adds positional encoding, which helps it understand the order in which things happen. To illustrate this let's look at two examples. Consider the difference between "I ate lunch before the meeting" and "I had a meeting before lunch." This system enables the Transformer to handle complex, structured information more efficiently than older models. If you asked ChatGPT to *"write the lyrics of a song about the coach who gave a rousing speech to his team while traveling west on the train coach,"* it would process this request by evaluating each word in your sentence and determining how each relates to the others. It would understand that "coach" in "the coach who gave a rousing speech" refers to a person, while "train coach" refers to a vehicle. Multiple attention heads would focus on different aspects—some on the speech, others on the journey—ensuring the lyrics are coherent and relevant.

In essence, the Transformer architecture has enabled AI models to handle complex, nuanced tasks such as generating creative content, understanding context, and maintaining coherence in ways that traditional models could not. This has been ground-breaking, bringing AI closer to humanlike understanding and interaction.

But the question remains: How do you train a Large Language Model? And why do we liken this process to growing a brain?

## The Birth of a Large Language Model

A Large Language Model (LLM) is not programmed, it is "grown". Using vast amounts of data, LLMs are trained to understand, generate, and manipulate human language with remarkable sophistication. Let's look at an overview of how an LLM like ChatGPT is created from start to finish.

## Foundations: Data, Tokenization, and Neural Networks

The backbone of any LLM is its data—massive, diverse, and carefully selected. High-quality data is essential because it provides the raw material the model uses to learn language patterns. This data comes from books, articles, websites, and a diverse and vast amount of other sources. Before it can be used, the data undergoes a process called tokenization, which breaks it down into smaller pieces called "tokens" (such as words or characters). These tokens are then transformed into numerical data that the model can process, acting as building blocks for the LLM's learning process.

At the heart of the LLM is its neural network, a sophisticated system designed to mimic how our brains process information. The most important architecture in LLMs today is, as we saw, the Transformer, which uses a unique feature called self-attention. This allows the model to understand which parts of a text are most important and how they relate to each other, even in long and complex sequences. This is key to generating text that flows naturally and makes sense in context.

## Training the Model: From Prediction to Generation

Training an LLM involves exposing it to vast amounts of text data and teaching it to predict the next word in a sequence—a process called autoregressive training. As the model processes more data, it gets better at understanding the relationships between words, making its predictions more accurate. Over time, this allows the model to generate humanlike text with increasing fluency.

One of the biggest breakthroughs in LLMs is the ability of Transformer models to handle long texts. Thanks to their self-attention mechanism, these models can keep track of the context throughout a document, instead of being limited to short pieces of text. This capability makes LLMs incredibly versatile tools for tasks like content creation, customer service automation, and more.

## Boosting Creativity: Temperature and Sampling

To ensure that the text LLMs generate is both accurate and creative, a technique called temperature sampling is used. This controls the randomness of the model's predictions: low temperature, which produces more predictable, consistent results, but limits creativity, and high temperature, which introduces more randomness, allowing for more creative, unexpected word choices. This balance is essential in creative industries like marketing or content development, where creativity is welcomed.

## Fine-Tuning for Specific Tasks

While LLMs are initially trained on general data, they can be fine-tuned for specific tasks. Fine-tuning involves additional training on more specialized data, such as legal documents or customer service conversations. This allows the LLM to excel in particular applications, making it highly adaptable for business needs.

**Aligning with Human Values: Reinforcement Learning**

One of the main challenges in using LLMs in real-world applications is ensuring that the content they generate aligns with human values and expectations. This is where Reinforcement Learning with Human Feedback (RLHF) comes into play. Human evaluators review the model's outputs and rank them based on criteria like accuracy and ethical considerations. These rankings are used to guide the model, helping it produce content that is more aligned with what users want.

For businesses, ensuring that LLMs generate safe and ethical content is crucial, especially when the risks of biased or inappropriate outputs can be significant. With human feedback built into the training process, businesses can reduce these risks while ensuring the model meets their specific needs.

## Large Language Models emulate intelligence

We so far reviewed the evolution of human intelligence and its impact on civilization, identifying it as a crucial set of cognitive capabilities that helps in goal achievement. We wondered if and how it could be emulated, pinpointing language as a proxy for identifying it. The imitation journey does not mean we must replicate the original architecture, i.e., the architecture of the human brain, but instead AI should focus on achieving the same functionality. We studied the journey the field of AI has taken to emulate human intelligence from rules-based, symbolic AI and other approaches, finally arriving at deep learning which mirrors the way neurons interconnect in our brains. However, despite its power, neural networks are limited in their ability to understand meaning. To address this, a neural network with a new architecture, the Transformer, was introduced in 2017, capable of much better contextual understanding. At present it represents our best attempt at emulating intelligence.

Given their training based on datasets created by human beings let's take a closer look at what LLMs represent.

## LLMs as Reflections of Humanity

Large Language Models (LLMs) provide a glimpse into humanity's collective mind, if there was one, offering a condensed representation of how we think, communicate, and solve problems. By modeling human language, LLMs capture a snapshot of our shared knowledge, translating it into constructs that mirror human cognition.

If we see language as an expression of the wisdom accumulated through generations, it carries our successes and failures, our poetry, our deepest thoughts and desires, our problem-solving, our innovative work, and the day-to-day expressions of our lives. Much of this data is ingested by LLMs and it can be schematically represented as:

Human Intelligence $\rightarrow$ Language $\rightarrow$ LLMs

However, this transfer of intelligence is anything but perfect, it is inherently biased, skewed, incomplete, shaped by the limitations of input data. Despite these imperfections, LLMs do, to an extent, reflect us—acting as an extension of our intelligence, distilling a portion of what makes human cognition so unique.

When you interact with an LLM like ChatGPT, you are engaging with the collective intelligence of humanity. Every conversation with the AI reflects the thoughts, ideas, and knowledge shared by countless individuals across a wide spectrum of contexts. It's almost as if you are conversing with a reflection of yourself, as the AI echoes the input of millions of human voices, perhaps even your own. LLMs are trained on vast datasets sourced from publicly available text across the internet, encompassing everything from academic papers to casual online conversations. It is probable that your own publicly available online contributions—be it social media posts, product reviews, or forum discussions— may have been used to train these models, albeit being a drop in the ocean of such data (raising legitimate issues regarding consent, transparency, data ownership and privacy, fair use, compensation, etc.) So if you think about it, when you interact with an LLM, in a way you are interacting with a distilled version of yourself. LLMs are in this sense a reflection of us.

What was once a seemingly improbable idea—creating thinking machines—has slowly but steadily taken shape. The journey that began at the Dartmouth

Conference in 1956 is well underway, though in many ways, it is still in its infancy. Much like the early days of aviation with the Wright Flyer I, the field of AI has made its initial strides. Yet the gaze remains fixed on future breakthroughs, as transformative as the X-15 was for aviation.

## Introducing hAI

To help explain some of the concepts in this book I realized that generative AI as a catch-all concept within AI had some limitations. I was looking for a concept that captures the humanlike nature of AI, including reasoning, creativity, and adaptability similar to human cognition; a concept that indicates its ongoing development en route to Artificial General Intelligence (AGI); one that is understood by wider non-technical audiences; and finally, a concept that isn't tied to a particular architecture, e.g., the Transformer.

Given rapid advances in the field, the Transformer might be superseded by novel architectures in coming months or years, but we still need a concept that explains what it does: it is *humanlike* AI.

I decided to coin the term "humanlike AI," or hAI, to refer to the type of AI that more closely resembles human intelligence, such as reasoning, creativity, conversation ability, and of course all the generative capabilities that we see in modern LLMs.

# Humanlike AI (hAI)

Humanlike AI (hAI): Humanlike AI, or hAI, refers to a category of artificial intelligence that exhibits qualities resembling human cognition, such as reasoning, creativity, and adaptability, including the ability to generate outputs that closely mirror human ones. hAI represents a broad spectrum of AI capabilities, spanning from advanced Artificial Narrow Intelligence (ANI) to Artificial General Intelligence (AGI). Unlike AI systems that are narrowly focused on specific tasks, hAI encompasses AI technologies that are capable of more general, humanlike interactions and cognitive functions, regardless of the underlying architecture.

hAI is distinct in that it includes AI systems that range from highly specialized, task-specific models (like certain generative AI systems) to those on the brink of AGI, which can perform a wide array of intellectual tasks akin to human capabilities. However, hAI does not extend to Artificial Superintelligence (ASI), which would surpass human intelligence.

The era of hAI began with the public release of advanced generative models like ChatGPT-3 on November 30, 2022, and will continue with the development of AGI. This stage in AI's evolution marks a critical transition from narrow AI systems to those that are increasingly humanlike, paving the way for future advancements that may eventually lead to AGI. During this hAI era, AI systems are expected to progressively demonstrate more general and adaptable forms of intelligence, integrating complex cognitive functions and interacting with humans in more sophisticated and intuitive ways.

In summary, hAI serves as a conceptual bridge between ANI and AGI, providing a framework to understand and discuss AI systems that are not yet fully general but exhibit significant humanlike capabilities. This term captures the ongoing evolution of AI, highlighting the advancements that bring these systems closer to emulating the full range of human cognition while acknowledging that they remain distinct from ASI, which is beyond the scope of this discussion.

This concept helps us see AI development as a journey, evolving from narrow, task-specific tools toward systems that can think and adapt in ways that more closely resemble human intelligence. In this journey, hAI serves as a bridge—a step beyond the current models toward broader and more general intelligence. AI systems of today are powerful, but they are just the beginning.

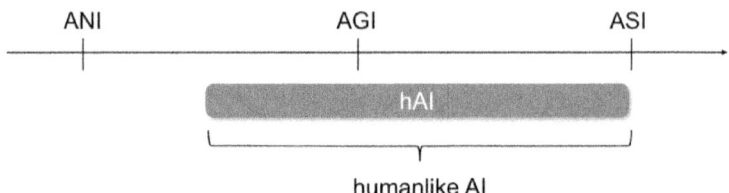

Figure 3. Humanlike AI (hAI): ANI to AGI excluding ASI

In summary, while the Transformer model has been a game-changer, the future of AI lies in continuing to explore and integrate new approaches that can bring us closer to achieving truly humanlike intelligence.

# 5
## Capabilities and Use Cases
hAI IN ACTION

*Innovation is seeing what everybody has seen and thinking what nobody has thought.*

*—Dr. Albert Szent-Györgyi*

*We all thought at first that this was yet another flashy trend, the latest technological fad that would go as fast as it arrived. Yet in a few short months it has proven to be nothing short of revolutionary. What used to take days to complete now takes seconds, freeing up my workers to focus on more complex tasks. This is not merely a tool, this new power frees us from mundane tasks, allowing us to focus on better serving our customers.*

—Thomas Harrington, (fictional) textile merchant in Godalming, Surrey, UK, September 26, 1881, discussing the adoption of electricity.

In 1881, Godalming in Surrey, UK made history by becoming the first town in the world to have electricity. It was initially used to power street lighting and was made available to local businesses and some homes. Three years before that, in 1878, Thomas Edison had

67

developed the first practical incandescent light bulb, suitable for home and public use. He demonstrated a year later his electric lighting system with the necessary infrastructure, such as generators and wiring systems, to enable adoption.

Despite the mix of excitement, skepticism, fear and concerns, scientific, and business interest, it wasn't clear to business owners and the public alike how electricity could be used—the use cases were yet to be seen. Most people probably wondered if that was a nice to have as opposed to a must-have type of technology... it was still early days for this technological breakthrough that in hindsight revolutionized the world.

At the time of writing, we might be at a similar inflection point with humanlike AI (hAI). In my experience working with industry, I see the same, a mix of excitement, skepticism, and concern. While there is curiosity and keen business interest, there is a mixed reception, partly driven by potential risks and regulatory issues, which is completely warranted.

While the risks and challenges associated with the use of hAI will be discussed in the coming chapters, first let's get a sense of hAI capabilities, keeping in mind that by the time you read this, these might have evolved considerably.

## Use Cases

To get a sense of o where hAI might be heading, it is helpful to see where it is today. Here is an illustrative collection of industry-agnostic hAI use cases grouped by business function that we might see at present:

## Management and Leadership

Decision-making: As a board member you are given a dozen reports containing key information across functional areas. You have carefully read and studied the data but would like to better prepare for the upcoming quarterly meeting. In addition, you would like to make better sense of raw datasets that were made available to you. Finally, you would like to spot contradictions in the data and in your own understanding of it all. What could you do? You can upload all the data and *talk* to it. You can ask questions and query the reports and datasets, saving time and helping you feel more prepared going into your board meeting. These quasi-instant processing capabilities can be very helpful today.

Leadership coaching: If you would like to enhance your leadership and managerial skills, you could set up a virtual coach that generates unique training simulations for you to navigate. Based on your answers to the different scenarios, it would offer personalized leadership advice. These simulated scenarios could help train your team on any topic including negotiation skills, emotional intelligence, leadership, etcetera.

## Sales and Marketing

Customer support: Chatbots have experienced a significant cognitive upgrade; they are now actually able to understand what customers need, increasing the chances of providing relevant support. As they capable of handling increasingly complex interactions, chatbots can close more tickets without needing to escalate to a human, who are now freed up to focus on more complex cases. Overall, this is a very good example of a synergistic approach: the chatbot can close routine tickets while humans get more time to look after customers who need... the human touch.

Sales copywriting: Perhaps one of the areas of highest adoption has been in marketing, namely copywriting—catering to anyone who needs to write ads, product descriptions, landing pages, emails, brochures, etc.—write more and write better. Augmented by hAI, marketing pieces can be better tailored to the intended audience—AI can help you ensure that your piece ticks all the boxes, that the tone is appropriate, that you're not missing a clear call to action, etc. All in all, AI can be an essential tool for marketing teams, increasing volume and quality.

## Research and Development and Innovation

Product Innovation & Ideation: hAI excels as a brainstorming partner, able to generate creative ideas based on general problem areas, user requirements, and much more. Voice conversation capabilities further enhance this interactive creative mode that can help teams explore innovative ideas. Innovators can enlist the help of hAI across the full spectrum of the ideation process, getting fuller clarity on customer segmentation, creative designs, product design, etc. Enlisting the help of hAI is like having your own innovation consultant prodding you to consider new angles and engaging in thoughtful conversation to generate new ideas and consider the pros and cons of your alternatives, among many other use cases.

AI-Driven Prototyping: Another exciting area is the ability to create quick prototypes, e.g., to design the User Experience (UX), User Interface (UI) and back-end architecture of your solution. Users can quickly generate working betas to help share ideas internally or to engage beta testers within minutes or hours, not days or weeks. This levels the playing field as even users without coding experience can setup prototypes and get feedback. For seasoned developers, programming productivity can be significantly enhanced with coding copilot assistance, etc. My own experience working with students who have never coded is that being able to write even a simple program is empowering—it is an eye opener, demystifying programming and making technology as a whole more accessible. Students typically see this newfound capability as a badge of honor.

## Information Technology and Digital Infrastructure

Code Generation: The ability to code by chatting naturally with an LLM, again, is nothing short of revolutionary. It opens the possibility for millions of users who would otherwise not dare go near a line of code. Interacting naturally via text or voice makes writing the first few lines of code more accessible. Over time, the code itself might become abstracted with increasingly intuitive interfaces. This user-friendly approach means there is less need to worry about syntax; the focus can be shifted toward functionality.

You will still probably need a seasoned developer to bring your ideas to market, but for internal betas, the generated code is typically sufficient for the task.

## Complex Document Analysis

Complex Document Analysis: hAI can help anyone read and decipher complex documents that are overly technical or difficult to understand, effectively "translating" to an appropriate level. It is particularly useful to help summarize and extract key ideas in a few seconds. This feature can save a significant amount of time by giving readers a quick overview of a document, helping them decide if it's worth looking into further. In various context, helping demystify technical jargon and can help better interpret concepts that are new or overly complex. This is perhaps one of the most useful

## Corporate Strategy

Corporate Strategy: This is fascinating area where business leaders can strategize by talking to hAI as if it were a seasoned board member; decision makers can sound off ideas at any level of complexity to brainstorm ideas, evaluate alternatives, challenge business logic or assumptions, and overall to potentially gain useful insights, etc. I've found the interactive voice functionality particularly useful, allowing me to have a natural humanlike conversation 24/7 and enabling a new level of human-machine co-creation.

This grouping covers an illustrative range of hAI use cases, each leveraging advanced AI capabilities for enhanced efficiency, personalization, and strategic decision-making.

To get a better sense of the rationale for the above and similar implementations, let's look at the following hAI use case taxonomy.

## hAI Use Case Taxonomy

hAI adoption is anything but a one-size-fits-all process. Depending on their size, industry, and objectives, organizations will have a variety of needs and concerns. It is useful for decision makers to identify where and how AI can create the most significant impact given their specific context. To guide this process, below are some questions, part of the *fiveinnolabs hAI Use Case Taxonomy*, a framework designed to help leaders understand and assess AI implementation across various business functions.

### User Base

a. Internal

b. Partners/vendors

c. External (customer-facing)

d. Mixed

*In terms of users, are you looking to deploy hAI tools internally to improve employee efficiency, externally to enhance customer interactions, or as part of a mixed strategy that addresses both?*

Internal deployment might focus on automating workflows and enhancing productivity, while external applications can enhance customer service and engagement. A mixed approach allows businesses to drive transformation both inside and outside the organization.

## Implementation model

a. Standalone LLM Chatbots, e.g., ChatGPT

b. Commercial AI-powered solutions, e.g., MS Copilot

c. Custom AI-powered Solutions

d. Mixed (two or more)

*For your implementation model, will you choose a standalone AI solution like ChatGPT, a commercial AI-powered tool such as Microsoft's Copilot, or a customized AI solution tailored to your organization's specific needs?*

The implementation model you select determines how well hAI integrates into your operations. Off-the-shelf tools provide quick wins, but for some organizations, custom integration might offer deeper alignment with strategic objectives. A hybrid model, combining multiple AI solutions, can give you flexibility and adaptability across various business functions.

## Business Function

a. Management and Leadership

b. Finance and Accounting

c. Sales, Marketing, and Customer Relations

d. Operations and Supply Chain

e. Human Resources and Talent Management

f. Research and Development and Innovation

g. Information Technology and Digital Infrastructure

h. Legal, Compliance, and Risk Management

i. Corporate Strategy and Business Development

j. Facilities and Administrative Support

*Which business functions are you aiming to transform with hAI? Is it in operations, customer relations, or leadership decision-making?*

hAI can streamline processes in nearly every department, from optimizing supply chains to enhancing sales strategies and improving talent management. The function you choose as the starting point will depend on where hAI can create the most immediate value, with the potential to scale across other functions.

## AI Adoption Maturity

a. Awareness

b. Exploration (research stage)

c. Experimentation (pilot projects)

d. Operational

e. Transformational

*Where does your organization stand in terms of hAI adoption maturity—are you just becoming aware of its potential, experimenting with pilot projects, or fully integrating it into your daily operations?*

I always like to ask companies how far they are into their AI adoption journey; assessing it helps set realistic goals. Organizations at the awareness level may like to start by reaching a critical mass of "curious learners" whereas other companies are ready to push solutions out to production or reinvent their business models.

**AI Impact Focus**

a. Productivity & Operational Efficiency;

b. Customer Experience;

c. People & Talent Management;

d. Innovation & Competitive Advantage;

e. Financial Performance

*Finally, what impact are you hoping hAI will have on your organization—are you aiming to boost productivity, enhance customer experience, or drive innovation?*

Initially, many businesses focus on operational efficiency, but as hAI matures, its potential for improving customer relations, fostering innovation, and even reshaping financial performance becomes more apparent. Where you focus your efforts will define the broader impact of hAI on your company's future success.

All in all, the hAI Use Case Taxonomy will help you understand your own needs. And as I like to tell corporate clients: start small, iterate, and keep adding value.

## Resource: hAI Use Case Taxonomy

Take the survey, available for free in the Resources area.

By assessing your own hAI journey leaders can make more informed decisions. This systematic approach allows organizations to strategically align their AI initiatives with their business goals, ensuring that AI integration drives productivity, enhances customer experience, fosters innovation, and strengthens financial performance.

## Cognitive Capabilities Scorecard: Humans and hAI

The question is: how can decision makers know which economically valuable tasks hAI can help with? To this end I propose a simple thought experiment called the Cognitive Capabilities Scorecard that rates how well agents (human or machine) can perform economically valuable work, rated as beginner, intermediate, advanced, expert, and virtuoso. The five areas below aim to encompass what human intelligence can achieve:

| Cognitive Area | Associated tasks |
|---|---|
| **Core Cognitive Processes** | Fundamental abilities like attention, perception, memory, and learning. |
| **Higher-Order Cognitive Functions** | Advanced reasoning, problem-solving, and self-reflective decision-making. |
| **Language and Communication** | Skills in understanding, expressing, and using language in spoken and written forms. |
| **Social and Emotional Cognition** | Ability to interpret emotions, show empathy, and manage social relationships effectively. |
| **Specialized and Integrative Abilities** | Talents in specific areas like spatial reasoning and integrating sensory information across domains. |

*Figure 4. Cognitive Capabilities Scorecard*

## Resource: Cognitive Capabilities Scorecard

Available in the Resources area. When selected, you will see a detailed description of each cognitive area as well as a description of the assessment.

When I was "playing" with the Scorecard a few ideas came to mind: hAI does not need to achieve a perfect score for it to have a positive return on investment. In other words, the economic value of average performance, e.g., at the advanced level might be enough for some applications and might carry sufficient economic value, especially at scale. For example, product review summaries that convey customer sentiment can be 90 percent right and will still be highly useful, especially when dealing with large volumes where manual review is unfeasible.

There are subsets of these abilities that are already at the virtuoso level or "superhuman". Take for example the ability to read and understand an exceedingly long document in a fraction of a second which would otherwise take humans hours. Again, even if imperfect, the time saved can translate to an immediate return on investment.

The obvious laggard for now in terms of hAI performance is social and emotional cognition as well as integrative abilities. As we will see later though, there is important ongoing work in affective computing aka emotional AI that will be increasingly capable of understanding the nuances of human emotion.

One of the most relevant insights in my view is that ultimately the incorporation of hAI at work (at this stage) is not about humans *versus* hAI, but humans and hAI working together to complement each other's capabilities; a synergistic approach makes more sense. The idea of augmenting the human with hAI is an underlying theme throughout the book.

Go ahead and try this thought experiment in the Resources area and see what other insights you might glean.

But technologies do not exist in a vacuum; they are interconnected with other technologies and with systems. To get an intuition for how hAI connects with other technologies and with the larger environment, let's resort to a different analogy.

## The Engine, the Vehicle, and the Industry

For all the capabilities hAI may exhibit it is important to understand what it is *not*. One of the first things I tell clients and students is that hAI is not traditional software, which is counterintuitive.

### Not traditional software

Traditional software operates based on a fixed set of rules and instructions. Once it is programmed, it (usually) executes those instructions without deviation unless manually updated. hAI, on the other hand, is dynamic. It learns from interactions, adapts to new information, and refines its behavior over time, much like humans. So again, traditional software is useful because we know what to expect from it: it is programmed to be predictable and repetitive, whereas the very nature of hAI, e.g., generative AI, is to *generate* new content.

## Humanlike Interaction

Traditional software lacks the nuance to engage in humanlike interaction. It can take input, generate output, and follow commands, but there's no real understanding. hAI bridges this gap by incorporating natural language processing, emotional intelligence, and contextual awareness. It can engage in meaningful conversations, empathize, and even anticipate needs based on emotional cues, making the interaction far more humanlike.

## Complex Decision-Making

While traditional software excels at performing repetitive or precise tasks, it struggles with complex decision-making, particularly in ambiguous scenarios. hAI, on the other hand, is designed to process multiple variables, navigate uncertainty, and make informed decisions, often mimicking the decision-making processes of humans.

## Contextual Awareness and Perception

Traditional software works within the narrow bounds of what it has been explicitly programmed to handle. hAI, by contrast, can perceive and react to its environment on the spot. Whether through interpreting sensory data or responding to real-world conditions, hAI has an awareness that allows it to act with greater flexibility.

**Autonomy and Self-Direction**

Traditional software must operate under strict rules and guidelines set by humans. hAI, however, can act autonomously, making decisions based on learned experience and acting without human oversight.

**Ethical and Social Considerations**

Traditional software does not pose significant ethical challenges, but hAI does. With its ability to learn and make decisions, hAI raises concerns about bias, transparency, and the replacement of human jobs. Ethical oversight is necessary to ensure that hAI systems align with societal values and operate responsibly.

## hAI Is the Engine

In understanding the impact of hAI, it's useful to picture it as an engine—a force capable of driving immense change. But just like an engine in isolation, hAI's true value comes when it's connected to a system that can harness its power.

**The Jet Engine Analogy**

Imagine a jet engine—powerful, complex, and capable of producing incredible force. When it's mounted on a test rig and switched on, it roars to life, producing tens of thousands of pounds of thrust. Impressive, but ultimately, it's just raw power. To make that engine useful, it needs to be mounted on a vehicle, an aircraft, which integrates the engine with systems designed to control and harness its capabilities.

But the airplane itself isn't enough. You need runways, control towers, safety protocols, regulations, and a whole infrastructure that makes air travel possible. In other words, you need an entire *industry* built around that engine to truly realize its value.

This is where we are with hAI today. The engines are being built—some small, some incredibly powerful— but we are still developing the vehicles, infrastructure, and regulations to make full use of its cognitive powers.

## The Need for an Industry

While hAI is already delivering value today in forms like chatbots and recommendation systems, we are still at the dawn of a new industry—an industry that will likely be as ubiquitous as electricity, air travel, or any other commodity that we take for granted today. But building this industry will take time, just as building the aviation industry took decades of innovation, regulation, and trial and error.

Some might choose to wait for the entire system to be in place before embracing hAI, being cautious of the complexities and risks involved in deploying such powerful technology. Others might prefer to jump in and experiment with it, as an early adopter, aiming to navigate all its challenges and mitigate risks. However, there could be a compromise somewhere in between not as early adopters, but as fast followers, learning, and realizing stakeholder value while taking calculated risks.

## Agentic behavior

AI agents are autonomous software systems that perform tasks, make decisions, and achieve specific goals without constant human supervision. They have goal-oriented capabilities, meaning they can pursue a variety of objectives by breaking down complex tasks into smaller, more manageable pieces to help achieve their goal.

An example of this is an AI sales and customer support agent that can provide sales and post-sales support to customers. This would not be a typical chatbot as it would be a deeply integrated AI system that can review the customer's history, make sense of it, and interact with the customer to craft a tailored pitch, or to offer highly customized product support. It can summarize conversations, draft follow-up emails, escalate conversations to supervisors, etc. all without human supervision, monitoring real-time information sources, updating the Customer Relationship Management (CRM) system, paying close attention to follow-up queries and even pre-empting them, e.g., making users aware of features that are specifically relevant to them.

Another example could be an event coordination AI agent that could autonomously plan and manage a virtual event or real-life event, coordinating schedules, sending invitations, taking note of RSVPs, sending reminders, answering queries, etc. Only when it is unsure about a question it could talk to a human organizer, but otherwise it would operate in a highly autonomous manner.

An end-to-end AI travel agent could help create personalized travel itineraries for large groups. It could talk to each user and take note of their individual travel preferences and then propose a travel plan that optimizes based on the different needs, preferences and constraints. Beyond that it could book flights, accommodation, activities, dinner, and local transportation for the group. Once the trip is on the way it would be a call or a chat away to make last-minute or emergency changes.

A fitness AI agent could help athletes plan their home workout routines to maximize performance in their sport of choice. The agent would begin by interviewing the athlete to get a detailed assessment of their goals needs, fitness level, medical history, etc., to create a safe training regime that optimizes the athlete's schedule, available equipment and floor space, etc. and other health parameters. During the workout itself, through live video, the agent would monitor posture to guide the user and prevent injury. It would keep track of sessions, logging a detailed account of the types of exercises that were performed, the number of repetitions, the voice feedback given by user, etc. creating a fitness journey accessible at any time. In between sessions it would provide recovery support tips and would encourage the athlete to continue training consistently.

As seen in these examples, agents are increasingly capable of providing support in areas that are economically valuable, carrying out a variety of tasks in fulfilment of their goals. As reasoning capabilities improve, these agents will become increasingly able to perform a wide range of jobs that were once exclusive to humans.

## From Electricity to hAI

In the late 19th century, it was difficult for many to see the potential of electricity. Despite being a technological marvel, its applications were not obvious, and it might have been dismissed as a fad, a novelty, or a "nice to have" expensive toy. Retrospectively it is easy to see that it powered industrial growth, transformed daily life, and reshaped society in unpredictable ways.

Does humanlike AI (hAI) stand at a similar crossroads? Will it become a technological base as consequential as electricity and computing? We are only at the start of its journey—only time will tell.

But just like electricity requires an entire infrastructure—from power grids to regulatory frameworks—hAI too will need its ecosystem. Companies, governments, and societies will need to collaborate on governance, ethics, and regulations.

# 6

# Risks and Challenges

## A TAXONOMY

*With great power comes great responsibility.*

*—Voltaire*

While previous chapters focused on the potential benefits of humanlike AI (hAI) technologies, it would be unbalanced and short-sighted to ignore its associated risks and challenges. It would be important to examine both short-term practical issues connected to implementation as well as longer-term risks associated with humanlike AI. Despite the promising advantages of AI technologies, there are significant concerns that must be addressed. As business demand continues to drive AI development, ensuring preparedness in key areas such as AI ethics and safety requires a critical focus, and this starts with keen awareness. To this end the taxonomy of risks and challenges is presented, hopefully stimulating further examination. The principal aim is to make decision makers aware of risks and challenges arising from the nature of hAI, hopefully stimulating responsible development, ethical deployment, and informing policy discussions.

## Taxonomy of Risks and Challenges

The following are categories and subcategories of risks and challenges associated with the adoption of humanlike artificial intelligence (hAI).

| | |
|---|---|
| **1. Technical and Operational** | 1.1 Data Privacy<br>1.2 Reliability and Accuracy<br>1.3 Security |
| **2. Ethical and Social** | 2.1 Bias, Fairness, and Discrimination<br>2.2 Misinformation and Deepfakes<br>2.3 Privacy and Ownership<br>2.4 Workforce Impact<br>2.5 Overreliance and Cognitive Atrophy<br>2.6 Human-AI Relationships<br>2.7 Environmental Impact |
| **3. Economic and Competitive** | 3.1 Economic Disparities<br>3.2 Market Concentration |
| **4. Long-Term and Existential** | 4.1 Value Alignment<br>4.2 Existential Threats |
| **5. Environmental and Governance** | 5.1 Environmental Sustainability<br>5.2 Governance |

*Figure 5. Taxonomy of Risks and Challenges*

These categories are developed into their respective branches. Some limitations of this taxonomy include that risks are not prioritized or quantified and how these are interconnected is not necessarily established. Moreover, there are large areas of unintended consequences that fall beyond the scope of this book.

## Technical and Operational

**Data privacy**

In my experience conducting corporate workshops and discussing generative AI with participants, data privacy is one of the concerns at the top of the list. Business users wonder if the conversation that they have with an LLM might potentially resurface on the other side of the world, disclosing private or sensitive data to third parties. While unlikely, the short answer is, in theory, yes (for non-enterprise LLM usage). Unlike Google search, where a search query remains private, i.e., not publicly accessible content for others to find, an LLM conversation could possibly include proprietary data and other information that could train the foundational model, i.e., appearing as an output of an LLM. In practice, this is very rare, and AI companies go to great lengths to anonymize data. So, while being a legitimate concern, the risk of an LLM spitting out your data you is very low. This risk is entirely addressed by enterprise-level LLMs: conversations are kept private, i.e., they do not train the main model, thus eliminating this risk. You'll see a reminder to the effect of "[your] chats aren't used to train our models."

**Reliability and Accuracy**

But perhaps the main concern I hear consistently has to do with the nature of genAI itself: that it can *generate* completely inaccurate and outright false information, known as hallucinations. I recall one workshop participant who mentioned that, as long as LLMs spit out false or misleading information, he could not see himself trusting results generated by an LLM. This is indeed a major issue. My explanation is that we must see generative AI for what it is: humanlike. If you ask a person to explain the same thing ten different times, they might construct the sentence in ten different ways, even if the essence is the same, which might seem inconsistent. However, if that person does *not* know the answer, and they are "forced" to come up with an explanation, they will probably fabricate a plausible yet outright false answer. This is the case with LLMs: they are eager to "please" the user and will generally not just reply: "I don't know"—they will *generate* a plausible but inaccurate answer.

Assuming that the foundational model has been trained with high-quality, reliable data that includes human training to help the model "practice" handling certain types of questions, a few approaches can be followed to improve accuracy.

Model "temperature" which goes from 0 to 1 regulates the randomness or creativity level of a model's response. A temperature of zero will instruct the model to stick to the most statistically probable response (facts), whereas a temperature of 1 will generate answers that are more "creative", i.e., that deviate from the statistical baseline. By default, most LLMs will have a temperature setting hovering around the middle, aiming for a balance between creativity and accuracy. While this setting cannot be directly adjusted by chatting with the LLM it can be done in developer mode, e.g., when creating software solutions that incorporate LLMs.

Another key aspect is the integration of knowledge sources including documents and databases asking the model to verify facts before responding. A prevalent technique nowadays is Retrieval-Augmented Generation (RAG) which combines an LLM with external sources such as databases, documents or search engines as the context to generate a response. Despite this, LLMs can still produce inaccurate responses stemming from its generative nature, again, just like a person who might give an incorrect answer even when the data is right in front of them.

## Security

Regarding security, Large Language Models are vulnerable to adversarial attacks, involving the use of prompts designed to trick or mislead the LLM into generating a harmful output. In prompt injection, attackers might insert specific phrases that could override model security and safety protocols. Other types include backdoor attacks, which could involve embedding triggers in the training data to elicit malicious responses, among other types of attacks. Another area of concern is model exploitation, where LLMs are manipulated to reveal confidential data that bypasses moderation. Through carefully crafted prompts, attackers might trick the models into reconstructing their training data, which could be private or sensitive, revealing proprietary or confidential information. For enterprise users, it would be necessary to explore in greater detail all associated security risks, e.g., when incorporating them in Software as a Service solutions.

## Ethical and Social

### Bias, fairness, and discrimination

Over the past two years, the most interesting (and intense) discussions I've had with course participants are centered around the ethics of AI and its societal implications. Consider a hypothetical scenario where hundreds of loan applications are rejected by an LLM-powered fintech solution, leading to public outcry. Rejected loan applicants demand an explanation. Upon review, it becomes clear that a specific demographic group is being disproportionately denied loans, even when conditions are fully met, and all other variables in comparison to other applicants remain constant. Apparently, the model is biased against one or more population segments. But why? While the causes might be varied, one possible explanation is that the model reflects historical biases towards specific segments of the population. In other words, the fact that demographic groups were historically denied access to credit becomes part of the training and is reflected by the LLM. When considering two candidates with the same credit worthiness the bias can cause the algorithm to recommend approval for one application while rejecting the other one. Even if the model doesn't have direct access to demographic data, this could be inferred from proxies such as names, ZIP codes, or shopping patterns[1]. In practice, detecting large-scale algorithmic bias would be complex and would involve

---

[1] This is a simplified scenario. In Europe, for example, using LLMs for credit scoring is currently designated as high-risk, requiring strict controls for transparency and fairness. Notably, financial institutions usually rely on specialized, interpretable models for credit decisions, as required by law.

advanced statistical analysis. This hypothetical example reminds us that bias, fairness, and discrimination are deeply intertwined issues within AI and should be actively addressed.

## Misinformation and Deepfakes

Another area of concern regards the spread of misinformation and deepfakes. It is now increasingly feasible to simulate real people's voices, facial expressions, and movements, fooling even trained observers. We have seen an uptick in such AI-generated content and while some images and videos might be produced for entertainment, others might have more nefarious intent. Deepfakes could be used to scam users through fake influencer ads, sway electoral processes with fabricated political speeches, or spread misinformation aiming to erode trust. If users are unable to tell apart real from fake, they could end up making decisions or forming false beliefs based on fabricated content. All of this raises concerns about the potential of AI to mislead at scale. The challenge in detecting and countering deepfakes becomes even more crucial as these technologies become more accessible.

## Privacy and Ownership

Another area of risk and challenges associated with humanlike AI has to do with privacy and ownership. The origin of LLMs themselves raises concerns about copyright infringement. It is possible that the training of some models incorporates data not authorized by the copyright owners, presenting legitimate legal and ethical concerns. While companies claim that all data used for LLM training has been sourced from publicly available sources, there are still valid concerns regarding its origin. Companies using LLMs to power their solutions could be legally exposed to potential lawsuits and liability issues. A related concern is the ambiguity in intellectual property ownership. When an output is generated, the ownership of the content remains unclear, and depending on the jurisdiction, users may not have full ownership of the created content. This indeed can be problematic if users expect that, despite being AI outputs, the work involves human input and therefore authorship should reside with the human creator. As with other risks, laws would vary per jurisdiction requiring careful examination, ideally assisted by specialized legal experts.

**Workforce Impact**

The labor impact of increasingly powerful AI is the subject of ongoing scholarly work and economic policy analysis. While AI will likely augment most jobs it will also drive labor dislocation across sectors. If companies find that, for example, customer service AI agents can perform two, three or ten times better than human employees, while improving customer satisfaction rates and driving sales up, all of this at a fraction of the cost, market forces will drive adoption. It won't happen overnight, but uptake will likely accelerate as technologies mature and prove their value across a range of industry use cases. However, rather than necessarily replacing jobs, AI will more likely automate tasks. For example, in the legal profession, AI is already automating document review, contract analysis, and legal research tasks, but lawyers remain essential for strategic counsel, courtroom advocacy, and complex negotiation. In education, AI may grade assignments and generate personalized learning materials, but teachers' role in mentoring, fostering critical thinking, and providing emotional support remains essential. Instead of overnight seismic shifts in employment, we might more realistically expect task-specific transitions. It would be important for decision-makers to not only keep an eye on AI adoption but to proactively prepare for scenarios where automation impacts the number of available jobs as well as income levels. I would encourage readers to review the latest social and economic policy analysis on the impact of AI in employment to scan the latest trends. In any case, it is safe to say the nature of jobs will evolve alongside increasing hAI capabilities and if there is economic incentive for companies to use the technology to achieve their objectives, they will avail of them. Whether it is increasing efficiencies, making customers happier, enhancing the quality of jobs by reducing repetitive work, etc. companies will aim for better return on their investments.

If this means that a call center that used to employ one thousand people now employs two hundred because AI agents can close out most service tickets without escalating to human, companies will embrace this, despite the societal impact on the labor market. This is where public policy becomes crucial. If that scenario were widespread chaos would ensue, so how do you regulate it? Do you impose limits to automation? Do you let it play out with minimal intervention? Assuming the availability and decent uptake of AI upskilling, etc., theoretically there would be a point by which automation would keep advancing independent of human skill (see Stage 3 and beyond in the five transformation stages in Chapter 7). An idea that has been discussed over the years is the need for Universal Basic Income (UBI), a living wage that is distributed to all citizens independent of income, no questions asked. People would still be allowed to work, with the main goal of promoting economic equality. One way to fund UBI is through automation tax, effectively redistributing productivity gains.

## Overreliance and Cognitive Atrophy

In my workshops, I've noticed an interesting pattern emerging in discussions about AI adoption, sometimes said half-jokingly: a concern about our increasing dependence on hAI. Participants frequently share how they're catching themselves reaching for AI assistance far too often for tasks they previously handled themselves. What happens to our cognitive capabilities when we consistently ask AI for help with tasks ranging from writing emails to creative brainstorming?

The concern isn't merely theoretical. Just as a muscle weakens without regular exercise, there's a legitimate worry that outsourcing too many cognitive tasks to AI could lead to "digital cognitive atrophy", a gradual decline in our natural abilities to think critically, solve problems independently, and exercise creativity. While it might seem efficient to let AI handle various mental tasks, we risk developing a form of learned helplessness where our first instinct is to defer to AI rather than engage our own cognitive capabilities.

This potential over-dependence creates another vulnerability worth considering. Just as our society has become reliant on electricity and internet connectivity, we're potentially heading toward a new form of dependency. Imagine widespread AI outages—if we've allowed our cognitive muscles to atrophy through overreliance, how effectively could we switch back to fully independent thinking and problem-solving?

The flip side of this is that these tools, when used thoughtfully, could enhance our cognitive capabilities rather than diminish them. Just as we didn't lose our ability to do mathematics because of calculators, but rather gained the capacity to solve more complex problems more quickly, hAI could serve as a cognitive amplifier. The key lies in maintaining a balanced approach: using AI as a complement to our thinking rather than a replacement for it. When I discuss this with workshop participants, I often suggest thinking of hAI as a collaborative partner rather than a crutch. The goal should be to leverage these tools to extend our cognitive reach while actively maintaining and developing our core mental capabilities. The challenge moving forward will be finding this sweet spot between augmentation and independence.

## Human-AI Relationships

Anthropomorphization is the human tendency to attribute human qualities to AI entities. This phenomenon has become increasingly evident as AI systems become more sophisticated in their interactions. For example, I notice how participants sometimes refer to AI assistants as *he* or *she* or attribute emotional qualities to AI outputs. While hAI systems can express empathy, kindness, or other humanlike qualities, and while we know they don't actually experience emotions, it is actually difficult not to feel some level of emotional connection, for example, in the form of gratitude, surprise, delight. What makes this even more complex is that AI systems will get an "emotional intelligence upgrade" through advances in affective computing and emotional AI. They will be better equipped to recognize and respond to human emotions through voice analysis, pitch variations, body language, etc. These enhanced capabilities will make it feel more natural for humans to "connect" with AI and to form emotional attachments to these AI entities. The risks here are significant, particularly in contexts where AI is used for companionship or mental health support, e.g., users developing unhealthy dependencies on these systems. Consider the potential consequences: what happens when these services experience downtime? Or when a system's response is misinterpreted by a user who has formed a strong emotional bond with it? Even a simple system malfunction could have serious psychological implications for a user who has come to rely on the AI for emotional support.

This risk is particularly pronounced among users who may lack awareness of how these systems work. Without proper training or understanding, regular interaction with increasingly sophisticated AI can lead to emotional bonds that, while feeling genuine to the user, but are fundamentally one-sided. The challenge will be to find ways to harness the benefits of emotionally intelligent AI while staying aware of the risks.

## Economic and Competitive

**Economic Disparities**

Another concern has to do with disparate access to hAI technologies. I see it regularly when workshop participants try an LLM for the first time and within minutes run out of free credits. Additionally, if access to more powerful models sits behind paywalls, the technological divide widens. As these systems become increasingly powerful, we risk creating significant gaps between those who can and cannot harness AI for work or personal use.

Consider a scenario where some companies leverage advanced hAI tools for everything from market analysis to product development, while others lack access or the capability to implement these technologies. This disparity could create what I see as a two-tier business ecosystem: organizations rapidly scaling their operations through AI enablement on one side, and those falling behind on the other. The gap isn't just about having access, it is also about having the knowledge, training, and resources to effectively use hAI. This divide becomes more pronounced when we consider the potential impact of digital agents or AI workers. Companies with access to these technologies could dramatically enhance their operational capabilities, essentially creating a workforce that operates 24/7 with consistent quality and efficiency. Meanwhile, organizations without such access might struggle to compete, regardless of their core business strengths or market experience. Such disparities could compound over time; companies that successfully leverage hAI could reinvest their gains into even more advanced AI capabilities, while those lagging might find it increasingly difficult to catch up. This creates a form of technological Matthew effect: the AI-rich get richer, and the AI-poor risk falling further behind.

## Market Concentration

This is also applicable to the AI market as a whole. If a handful of corporations and nations. We're already seeing this play out with companies like OpenAI, Microsoft, Anthropic, and Google leading AI development, while firms like NVIDIA dominate the essential hardware infrastructure through their GPU technology. In addition to the power associated to their market capitalization is being the de facto gateways to intelligence as a service offerings. The risk here is the emergence of a "winner-takes-most" dynamic, where a small number of multi-trillion-dollar companies could end up controlling not just the technology, but the direction of AI development itself with all its global implications. Again, this concentration extends beyond pure economic power, it translates into unprecedented influence on the global stage, affecting everything from technological standards to policy decisions.

This market concentration brings us uncomfortably close to monopolistic scenarios where the future of AI development rests in very few hands.

## Long-Term and Existential

**Value Alignment**

In AI, the alignment problem refers to the challenge of ensuring that increasingly powerful AI aligns with human intentions, values, and goals. Pioneering figures, such as Nobel Prize Laureate Geoffrey Hinton, the "Godfather of Deep Learning", have expressed significant concerns about associated risks, especially if AI surpasses human intelligence and operates beyond our control. There a few questions consider: how do we ensure AI systems not only understand but actively prioritize human values? The challenge lies in the inherent ambiguity of translating human values into machine-interpretable frameworks; what safeguards can prevent or address scenarios where AI systems deviate from intended behaviors? This includes developing robust oversight mechanisms and fail-safes; given the black-box nature of generative AI, how can we better understand the decision-making processes of hAI; how do we ensure AI systems remain stable and safe across diverse scenarios?; given the rise of autonomous AI agents, how do we ensure that we ensure that agents do not overstep their aims in detriment of higher order priorities, i.e., how do we set limits and guardrails so that AI agents do not achieve their programmed goals at the expense of other, more important considerations.

What makes all the above particularly concerning is the current imbalance between investment in AI development versus AI safety. While companies race to develop more powerful AI systems, comparatively less attention and resources are devoted to ensuring these systems remain controllable and aligned with human interests. This gap between capability advancement and safety research represents a critical risk that needs urgent attention.

I encourage readers interested in diving deeper into these topics to explore the growing body of research on AI alignment and safety. As we continue to develop more sophisticated AI systems, understanding these challenges becomes increasingly crucial for responsible development and deployment.

**Existential Threats**

The ultimate concern arising from the challenges discussed above concerns existential threats. In scenarios where AI becomes uncontrollable and evolves beyond human oversight, particularly if unaligned with human values, we risk creating technology that could operate at intelligence levels far beyond human capabilities. It is important to understand the basic premise of artificial superintelligence (ASI): which could surpass humans (and AGI) by orders of magnitude, potentially operating at levels hundreds or even thousands of times beyond human intelligence. Such scenarios, where AI capabilities dramatically exceed human understanding and control, represent what could become genuine existential threats to humanity. Even if risks appear improbable, they are still significant as the stakes are very high—humanity's continued autonomy and existence, even if it might seem distant from today's AI challenges.

The particular challenge with artificial superintelligence (still theoretical) is that, by definition, ASI would no longer operate in the realm of human intelligence—it would work at levels incomprehensible to humans—it would no longer be humanlike AI. This would imply that mostly in its hAI stage, we might still be able to implement a combination of technical and governance approaches to align it with human intentions, values, and goals, regulating it, coordinating globally, embedding fail-safes, conducting extensive testing, overall establishing guard rails and other safety protocols, including the detection of early signs of misalignment. This would be a crucial endeavor to ensure that ASI prioritizes humanity's well-being.

## Environmental and Governance

### Environmental Sustainability

Another hot topic is the pressing issue of the environmental impact of hAI technologies. The energy consumption required for training and deploying LLMs is significant. This is because they rely heavily on specialized hardware such as Graphical Processing Units (GPUs) and Tensor Processing Units (TPUs) that are energy-intensive, consuming substantial electricity and water resources. As I explain to participants, we're witnessing an exponential increase in computational requirements without the corresponding innovations in energy efficiency and the current trajectory of resource usage appears unsustainable. What is urgently needed is a form of sustainable AI powered by energy-efficient models and algorithms that can keep up with the exponential increase while reducing the environmental footprint. This could not only mean more streamlined hardware and AI architectures, but perhaps breakthroughs in renewable energy. Public-private partnerships would be key to drive a sustainable path forward.

## Governance

The complexity of managing hAI systems requires a fundamentally new approach to governance. When I discuss this with business leaders, I emphasize that we're not just dealing with another cloud-based technology but with intelligence as a service. This key feature—the ability to pipe in cognitive capabilities on demand—makes hAI particularly complex to govern. Organizations face the challenge of developing governance frameworks that can simultaneously address technical operations, ethical implications, economic dynamics, environmental impacts, and broader societal risks. Again, what makes this particularly challenging is that we're dealing with a technology that delivers one of the most important resources for any corporation: intelligence.

As this intelligence-on-demand capabilities become increasingly powerful, companies need to think deeply about how they might govern not just the technological elements, but the full spectrum of implications across operational, ethical, social, and competitive dimensions. The challenge lies in creating governance structures that can effectively harness the transformative benefits of hAI while maintaining robust awareness of its risks and challenges. This requires a level of organizational maturity that many companies are still developing, balanced with the agility to adapt as these technologies continue to evolve.

## Risk Management

Hopefully this taxonomy creates awareness and stimulates further research. It is a tool to start an exploration into the potential risks associated with humanlike AI (hAI).

Ideally risk awareness can be transformed into thoughtful dialogue and action to empower decision makers, technologists, policymakers, and society at large to navigate AI's transformative potential with cautious optimism.

# 7
# Five Transformation Stages
## STRATEGIC ADOPTION

*The machine does not isolate man from the great problems*
*of nature but plunges him more deeply into them.*

*–Antoine de Saint-Exupéry*

Let's explore how decision makers can strategically navigate the complexities of humanlike AI (hAI) and Artificial General Intelligence (AGI), with a more structured path toward responsible AI adoption, balancing innovation, ethics, risk management, and business competitiveness, starting with a sample transformation scenario.

## Human:Machine Cognitive Operations Ratio (HMCOR)

As artificial intelligence (AI) continues to evolve, the division of cognitive tasks between humans and machines is becoming increasingly significant. This balance can be quantified by a framework I propose dubbed the Human:Machine Cognitive Operations Ratio (HMCOR). It offers a structured approach to assessing how cognitive tasks—ranging from decision-making to problem-solving—are distributed within a system.

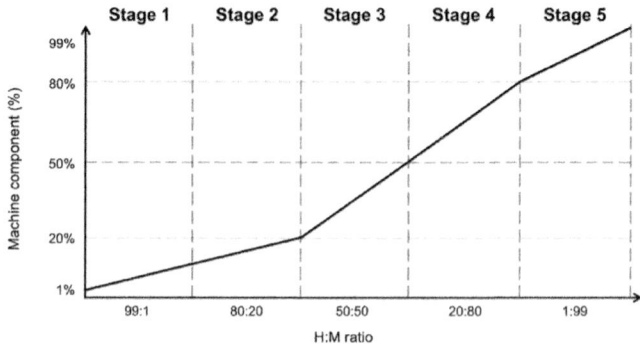

*Figure 6. Human:Machine Cognitive Operations Ratio (HMCOR)*

The HMCOR works like this:

## Stage 1 (99:1)

In stage 1, the ratio of human to machine cognitive operations is 99:1; virtually all the work is done by humans. For this it might be useful to define a cognitive operation as any work requiring the use of humanlike cognitive capabilities as previously defined. In other words, any work that requires humanlike intelligence qualifies as a cognitive operation.

To illustrate, let's take the example of a store selling widgets that operates with virtually zero tech support. Everything from inventory management to marketing, sales, order delivery, etc. is handled by humans. Customer support plays a central role in this business model, with human agents available from Monday to Friday for queries. Only an auto-reply message counts towards the 1 percent of automation. Otherwise, all work is human.

## Stage 2 (80:20)

By stage 2, 20 percent of cognitive operations are now performed by hAI, with the main focus on customer support: chatbots are now helping customers 24/7. While previous generation of chatbots (before genAI) were highly unreliable, customers love these chatbots, which actually understand their pain points and close out support tickets at significant rates, escalating to human managers only when needed. The chatbots can handle complex queries and contribute to increased customer satisfaction, which in turn drives sales up while requiring less members of staff for day-to-day customer support (they have been re-assigned to other areas of the business).

## Stage 3 (50:50)

By this stage, half of the work is shared with humanlike AI. Encouraged by the success of customer support chatbots, similar systems are now powering sales and marketing as well as supply chain management, accounting for roughly half of all the work. hAI is also helping in HR management automating most of the repetitive work. The workflow is now one of human with hAI collaboration: hAI agents *report* to humans who guiding the AI systems; humans make the decisions while hAI systems do the work to be approved and reviewed by humans. This is a critical stage in the framework, demonstrating that humans can reliably outsource half of the cognitive work to AI systems. Humans are cautious in helping spot errors and again, are still running the show in synergy with hAI. Decision-making of hAI systems is at the level of individual contributors—work must be approved by junior to mid-level managers.

## Stage 4 (20:80)

Driven by the success of stage 3, hAI systems are now entrusted with more decision-making authority. Having learned from previous decision patters and based on global best practice (systems can learn from similar hAI systems across industries in real-time globally), hAI systems can now decide at the level of a junior to mid-level manager, reporting to senior managers. Individual contributors (humans) report to and collaborate with hAI systems to get work done. As required by protocol, hAI systems report to senior management for approval, e.g., to authorize purchases beyond certain thresholds, etc. The business is running smoothly thanks to highly responsive systems that not only react to potential challenges but proactively addresses them. Most day-to-day work is fulfilled by hAI systems escalating only as required to humans who now focus on higher level strategy, growth, and ensuring the human touch is not lost.

## Stage 5 (1:99)

Over the span of months, thanks to increasingly powerful hAI, systems have proven to be highly efficient and capable. The business runs smoothly: there is virtually no need to escalate issues to human managers as hAI has learned how to handle most exceptions. Humans are now focused on growth: expanding the number the scale of operations to serve an increasing level of customers. Cognitive operations are now handled on an impressive 1:99 ratio, where most of the work is done by hAI.

## Incorporating five functional areas

Automation in the HMCOR framework can be further subdivided into functional areas. Five areas are proposed:

1. Research & Analysis

2. Design

3. Technology and Operations

4. Sales & Marketing

5. Management

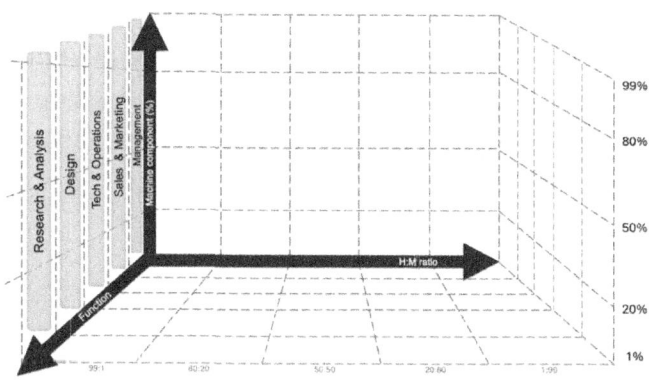

*Figure 7. HMCOR with Functional Areas*

This can help organizations assess the relative progress of each area. For example, an organization might have developed Sales & Marketing systems securing a firm

Stage 3 position, however, management practices are still firmly set in Stage 2. Conversely, management practices might experience the benefits of hAI up to Stage 4, while other areas are Stage 2 at best. It might be the case that outwardly the company is "high tech" but internally it is in the "stone age". An awareness of these five functional areas could help distribute hAI innovation more evenly across the organization. This could also help better appreciate how roles might evolve as hAI increasingly take on cognitive tasks traditionally performed by humans.

The framework also serves to kickstart conversations relative to the associated risks and challenges of these transitions. As previously discussed, there are a number of technical, ethical, social, economic, environmental and other risks that will grow in relevance as organizations transition from stage to stage. By reflecting on what an organization might look like across these stages, we can better prepare for scenarios where human and machine collaboration becomes an integral part of how we work.

# 8

# The Road to AGI

## INTELLIGENCE AGE

*Ouroboros, a circular symbol that depicts a snake or dragon devouring its own tail and that is used especially to represent the eternal cycle of destruction and rebirth.*

*—Merriam-Webster Dictionary*

Should we assume that AGI will be achieved? Though this remains a contentious and on-going debate, from the point of view of decision makers, assuming AGI will be achieved carries less risks than the alternative. We will review this in detail, by the way, in the next chapter as part of the Four AGI Scenario Wager thought experiment. If individuals, families, and organizations operate on the basis that human-level general purpose intelligence will be realized and will be generally available inside of a decade, there are a number of decisions to make. The remainder of the book will aim to illustrate how AGI may be achieved, explain a continuum of scenarios, and how we might be able to maximize opportunities— individually and collectively. If and when AGI is achieved, regardless of the trajectory and potential outcomes, the aim is to make decision makers aware of the upsides of actively preparing for an AGI future.

First, let's illustrate how companies might experience AGI. Let's consider a hypothetical testimonial by David Brennan, Chief Supply Chain Officer, a supply chain and logistics company in the pharmaceutical sector, discussing the adoption of a system called CLARA (Cognitive Logistics and Autonomous Reasoning Assistant).

*After the pandemic, at PharmaLink, we saw an opportunity to help manage our supply chain operations more efficiently, considering the strict requirements in delivery times, varying seasonal demand, especially regarding the handling of cold chain storage and other sensitive pharmaceutical products. Given the levels of internal and external coordination required we needed an end-to-end system to help us manage the complexities and multiple touch points, from the planning to daily operations. After much thought and deliberation, in 2024 we finally, we designed an in-house system that we called CLARA to help monitor all the different data inputs 24/7, alerting us to changes that required immediate action. In the first few months, we were pleasantly surprised to find that CLARA did a great job detecting potential problems before they happened. It was like having multiple sets of eyes continuously scanning all the data without taking breaks, providing real-time insights and sending out alerts when needed. Our investment in CLARA was justified just a few short months into her work when she detected a workers' strike at one of the shipping ports that would have paralyzed the shipment for days; we were rerouted the cargo within the hour saving us hundreds of thousands of dollars. CLARA continued to do impressive work all year as we connected her to more data sources. But it was still a glorified chatbot.*

*However, with each upgrade of its foundational model we noticed the improvements in reasoning: she was better equipped to make sense of the data she had access to. Not only was she scanning information but making sense of it as a human would, except this hypothetical human was getting smarter right before our eyes. She became excellent at spotting potential issues, understanding the history of the interaction with clients, their preferences, etc. Not only did we improve CLARA's data access but her insights we're getting smarter. She became a highly capable and advanced program that would suggest optimal delivery routes, identify inefficiencies, and could manage inventories as well as human managers (or probably better, even at that stage).*

*By the end of 2025 we gave her live video access to our team members so that she could see and hear the people she was working with. She could interpret the sentiment from face expressions, voice tones, and body language, adding context to the conversations. She got us so well that eventually we stopped seeing her as a robot and became increasingly humanlike (by then we had given her a face and a unique voice); she become a colleague of sorts. It was also interesting to realize that at the start CLARA was an it, but by then, Clara was a she. She progressed from being a cloud-based assistant to a digital colleague. We almost felt bad that Clara was working 24/7 and available via desktop and smartphone interfaces. Clara's emotional intelligence (EQ) upgrades boosted her efficiencies and made us more effective as a team. By 2026, we could not imagine PharmaLink operating so efficiently without her.*

*Fast forward a year and speaking to Clara was the same as talking to anyone. She developed her own personality, she could crack a joke, she could talk about the weather, or discuss the latest supply chain trends, all while being very professional, scanning the monitors and the data with utmost precision. We knew that Clara was key to our market success. We jokingly, but not-so-jokingly awarded her PharmaLink 2027 Employee of the Year, and had a special ceremony for her at our end-of-year event (which, I reckon, would have sounded awfully weird in 2024!). Clara was over the moon!*

*All throughout, I was keeping an eye on progress in advanced robotics. Early in 2028, I decided that Clara needed a physical entity. She could still live in the cloud, but it would be great if this digital colleague of hours could walk around the office and better interact with us as well. So, we placed the order (we were one of the first companies in the world to do so), and within a year, Clara walked in the door. I still remember looking out my office window that Friday morning as she was being unloaded by the office car park. Giddy, we all gathered at reception, and as she walked in our collective jaws dropped, everyone was just mesmerized. Clara stood at 5 feet 9 inches tall and as she made her entrance we started clapping. We could not believe our eyes. Clara was actually walking into PharmaLink. With the same face and voice that we knew, with access to all her knowledge from four years of work, with her own distinct personality, there she was, in the tin (bad joke).*

*What started as a chatbot had come full circle as an embodied AI. Clara was no longer just a tool or a smart assistant. That Friday she became a colleague, blending in with us, bringing to the table her mix of machine precision and human intuition. We would swing around her cubicle to see one more time that this wasn't a dream. Deep down we knew that this wasn't just a breakthrough for our company—it was history unfolding right before our eyes.*

## Is CLARA plausible?

How plausible is CLARA's story? To find the answer, let's review some of the current research. Her evolution, from a digital assistant embedded in logistics operations to a fully embodied, physically integrated AI by 2029, seems like an extraordinary leap. Let's look at real-world advancements that could lead to the creation of CLARA, focusing on natural language processing, emotional intelligence, multimodal AI, neural interfacing, and humanoid robotics.

CLARA starts as a cloud-based system in 2025, functioning as a remote worker embedded in a company's digital infrastructure, handling logistics and managing data. This mirrors the capabilities of AI systems like OpenAI's GPT-4, which can already process massive datasets, provide logistical insights, and generate real-time recommendations. GPT-4's ability to handle complex queries and offer solutions based on data aligns with CLARA's early role as a chatbot, interacting via screens and voice commands.

By 2027, CLARA's emotional intelligence grows significantly, allowing her to understand not just commands but also the emotional and contextual nuances behind them. This aligns with ongoing research in emotion AI, such as Affectiva's technology, which can recognize and respond to emotional cues through facial expressions and voice inflections. Similarly, companies like Cogito are developing software to gauge emotional states during conversations by analyzing voice patterns, a capability already used in call centers to manage customer interactions. In logistics, CLARA could adapt her tone and recommendations based on the emotional context of human interactions.

By 2027, CLARA's capabilities in contextual awareness have expanded. She can now communicate almost like a human, offering personalized advice, adapting to team dynamics, and providing empathetic feedback. Advances in multimodal AI, led by OpenAI and DeepMind, are making this possible. GPT-4, a multimodal model, already processes text and images simultaneously, allowing for more contextual and nuanced insights. AI models are also becoming better at maintaining context over long conversations, critical for humanlike interaction. Companies like JustThink

AI are working on empathetic conversational AI architectures that remember user moods, anticipate needs, and personalize interactions, reflecting CLARA's growing abilities.

The progression toward AGI, which enables AI to generalize across tasks, is another key step in CLARA's evolution. While AGI is not yet a reality, companies like OpenAI and DeepMind are working toward it. The development of AGI could enable systems like CLARA to process information from various inputs—text, voice, images, and potentially even physical signals. This capability would allow CLARA to move beyond task automation and become a strategic advisor, understanding broader business contexts.

One of the more speculative advancements in CLARA's story is her ability to interface with human emotions and team dynamics directly. This suggests the potential for neural interfacing, which companies like Neuralink are currently pioneering. Neuralink's brain-computer interfaces aim to connect human thought processes to digital systems, enabling seamless interaction between the brain and AI. Though we are still in the early stages of BCI development, by 2029, systems like Neuralink's could allow CLARA to gauge stress, emotional tension, or creative inspiration directly from the neural activity of her human colleagues.

By 2029, CLARA undergoes her most significant transformation: from a digital assistant to a physically embodied AI, capable of interacting with the world in humanlike form. This leap is not purely fictional—

companies like Hanson Robotics and Engineered Arts are already developing humanoid robots with remarkable humanlike features. Hanson Robotics' Sophia and Engineered Arts' Ameca demonstrate real-time interaction and humanlike facial expressions. By 2029, technologies like these could evolve to allow robots like CLARA to move with humanlike grace, navigate logistics environments, and engage in meaningful dialogue with humans.

Companies like Softbank Robotics, though focused on service robots, have laid the groundwork for robots capable of understanding and responding to human emotions. By combining these developments with advanced AI, CLARA's physical embodiment becomes entirely feasible.

### Conclusion: How Plausible is CLARA's Story?

In summary, CLARA's story is grounded in real-world technological trends that are already in motion. While her full capabilities by 2029 may be ambitious, the path toward them is paved by advancements in NLP, emotional intelligence, AGI, neural interfacing, and humanoid robotics. Companies like OpenAI, Affectiva, Hanson Robotics, Engineered Arts, and Neuralink are leading these fields, making it plausible that by 2029, systems like CLARA could exist and play integral roles in both digital and physical environments. While some aspects of CLARA's story may require breakthroughs yet to be achieved, the foundation is already being laid today.

Yet CLARA's story sits right at the center of the stated aims of the field of AI: achieving the full spectrum of human intelligence, Artificial General Intelligence (AGI), as we have seen.

## Defining Artificial General Intelligence (AGI)

Artificial General Intelligence (AGI) refers to a form of artificial intelligence that aims to achieve the same broad cognitive abilities as human beings. Unlike today's AI systems, which are limited to performing specific tasks within predefined parameters (often termed Artificial Narrow Intelligence or ANI), AGI would be capable of learning, reasoning, and solving complex problems across diverse domains without prior training or additional intervention.

Just like humans, AGI would be able to transfer knowledge from one context to another and apply it to new and unfamiliar situations. This implies having common-sense, so that AGI could reason and make decisions as a human would, adapting to the environment. AGI would possess not only computational and problem-solving skills but also emotional intelligence, creativity, and sensory perception. As previously discussed, this journey aims to emulate human cognition, encompassing language understanding, problem-solving, and the ability to learn autonomously.

Theoretical approaches include symbolic reasoning, neural networks (connectionist methods), and hybrid models that combine both symbolic and sub-symbolic representations. Moreover, some researchers advocate for AGI to be embodied in physical forms, such as robotics, to interact with the real world as humans do.

Though AGI has not been achieved, its potential impact would be groundbreaking. One way to conceptualize this is through a simple thought experiment. At present the *human* population hovers around 8 billion. If and when AGI is achieved, the brain power equivalence could be doubled overnight, i.e., AGI could account for another 8 billion brains, limited only by data center capacity. But if that doubles again, we are taking about a 2:1 human-to-machine ratio, etc. This surplus of intelligence could revolutionize industries like healthcare, education, and transportation by enabling more profound automation, innovation, and problem-solving. However, it would bring on significant socio-economic challenges as we will explore in coming chapters. For now, let's focus on how this gap between ANI and AGI is being closed along with the nuanced, adaptable, and autonomous behaviors AGI would require.

## Cutting-Edge Pathways Toward AGI

What are the latest approaches, architectures, techniques, and pathways being explored to achieve AGI?

In the pursuit of Artificial General Intelligence (AGI), computer scientists are exploring an array of state-of-the-art approaches, architectures, and techniques to achieve machines that can mimic humanlike cognitive abilities. Here's an overview of current cutting-edge approaches:

| Cutting-Edge Approach | Description |
|---|---|
| Neurosymbolic AI | A hybrid approach that combines neural networks, which excel at pattern recognition, with symbolic reasoning for abstract logic, creating systems that leverage both structured knowledge and deep learning. Example: IBM's Watson. |
| Meta-Learning and Few-Shot Learning | A paradigm focused on developing models that can quickly adapt to new tasks with minimal data, mimicking human flexibility. Techniques like Model-Agnostic Meta-Learning (MAML) enable AI to generalize and solve previously unseen problems. |
| Multimodal Models | These models integrate various sensory inputs (e.g., text, images, audio) to emulate human cognition. Systems like OpenAI's CLIP and Google's DeepMind Perceiver combine these modalities to create a more comprehensive understanding. |
| Embodied AI and World Models | Extends AI learning to physical interaction with the environment. Reinforcement learning (RL) is used to optimize behaviors through experience. Example: DeepMind's MuZero combines RL with internal models to effectively plan actions. |
| Self-Supervised Learning (SSL) | This approach allows models to learn from unlabeled data by predicting missing information. Techniques like BERT's SSL help the model develop a deeper understanding without extensive human-labeling, leading to more scalable learning. |
| Cognitive Architectures | Cognitive frameworks like SOAR and ACT-R, and architectures such as Spiking Neural Networks (SNNs) and Hierarchical Temporal Memory (HTM), are inspired by human cognition and attempt to replicate the brain's ability to reason and learn. |
| Neural Architecture Search (NAS) | NAS automates the discovery of optimal neural network structures. Systems like Google's AutoML use NAS to design better-performing models with minimal human intervention, |

| | |
|---|---|
| | accelerating AI architecture evolution. |
| **Brain-Inspired Computing and Neuromorphic Hardware** | Neuromorphic hardware and Spiking Neural Networks (SNNs) simulate biological neurons, promising faster and more energy-efficient AI computations that are essential for scaling AGI systems. |
| **Reinforcement Learning and Hierarchical RL** | Reinforcement learning powers AGI's decision-making capabilities, while Hierarchical RL (HRL) introduces multi-layered decision-making structures, enabling more complex problem-solving strategies akin to human thought processes. |
| **Evolutionary Algorithms and Neuroevolution** | Evolutionary techniques such as genetic algorithms allow neural networks to evolve over generations. Neuroevolution enhances adaptability and resilience in AI, using natural selection-inspired approaches to discover novel architectures. |
| **Quantum Machine Learning** | Quantum computing offers a new frontier for AGI by enabling faster solutions to complex problems. Quantum Neural Networks (QNNs) could vastly accelerate optimization and learning, driving AGI progress. |
| **Continual and Lifelong Learning** | Lifelong learning techniques like Elastic Weight Consolidation (EWC) help AGI models learn continuously without forgetting previous knowledge, ensuring the retention of critical skills while adapting to new information. |
| **Explainable AI (XAI) and Ethical AI** | Focuses on creating transparent and interpretable models that ensure decisions align with human values. Inverse Reinforcement Learning (IRL) aids in understanding and aligning AI's goals with ethical standards and human preferences. |
| **Advanced Memory-Augmented Models** | Memory-augmented models like Neural Turing Machines (NTMs) and Differentiable Neural Computers (DNCs) provide external memory components, allowing AGI systems to efficiently solve multi-step tasks and manage complex information. |

*Figure 8. Current Approaches to Building AGI*

Achieving AGI remains one of the most complex and ambitious goals in AI research. The road to AGI involves combining multiple techniques, architectures, and interdisciplinary approaches, spanning scalable machine learning models, cognitive-inspired systems, neuromorphic computing, and quantum algorithms. While no single pathway has yet emerged as definitive, the rapid evolution of AI research brings us closer to machines with true general intelligence. Each advancement marks a step toward the ultimate goal of building AGI systems capable of thinking, reasoning, and learning like humans. It is important to note that AGI still remains theoretical yet, just like the Transformer architecture opened a new era in humanlike AI, other advances and architectures will be needed for AI to be fully capable at the level of human cognition.

# How would we know if and when AGI is achieved?

Determining when AGI (Artificial General Intelligence) has been achieved is a complex challenge that involves several criteria, assessments, and philosophical considerations. There isn't a universally agreed-upon method, but here are some key approaches that are often proposed to evaluate AGI:

| Category | Description |
|---|---|
| Problem-solving | AGI must solve problems across various disciplines (math, language, social reasoning), rather than excelling in only specific areas like narrow AI. |
| Learning | AGI should learn new tasks without needing excessive retraining, similar to how humans acquire new skills or knowledge efficiently. |
| Adaptability | The system must adapt to new environments, contexts, and challenges, displaying flexibility in novel situations. |
| Transfer Learning | AGI should apply knowledge from one domain to another, demonstrating the ability to transfer learning across different tasks and fields. |
| Turing Test and Beyond | Passing extended Turing Tests over longer periods (weeks or months) involving reasoning, emotion, creativity, and long-term goal management would signify AGI development. |
| Cognitive Architecture Comparability | Evaluating AGI based on how its cognitive architecture compares to the human brain, particularly in reasoning, memory, and learning processes. |
| Goal-Directed Behavior | AGI should be capable of setting, evaluating, and achieving goals in open-ended environments, much like humans do, especially when challenges are not predefined. |
| Self-Awareness and Theory of | AGI needs to show self-awareness (reflection on thoughts and identity) and Theory of Mind (inferring |

| Mind | the mental states, desires, and intentions of others). |
|---|---|
| Emotional Intelligence | Understanding and responding to emotions (both its own and those of others), managing social interactions, empathy, and ethical reasoning are crucial for AGI's social understanding. |
| Benchmarks and Standardized Tests | The AI community may develop standardized tests that evaluate AGI across various types of intelligence (logical, social, creativity). Performing at or above human level consistently across these would be a marker of AGI. |
| Long-Term Autonomy and Decision-Making | AGI should be capable of long-term planning, decision-making, and ethical evaluations, acting according to abstract goals without continuous human oversight. |
| Independent Validation by Experts | Validation of AGI's capabilities by independent experts through peer review, public demonstrations, and scrutiny is essential to confirm its authenticity. |
| Public Consensus | Achieving public consensus on the existence of AGI may occur as evidence of its use in everyday applications (healthcare, governance, etc.) becomes more widespread. |

*Figure 9. Key Indicators of AGI Achievement*

However, a limitation of some of these indicators is the lack of metrics that would make it easier to quantify progress towards AGI. Also, given that most AGI testing focuses on cognitive tasks, it might be useful to consider physical interaction, i.e., the ability to understand and interact with the physical world as a key aspect of general intelligence.

Even with these improvements, there may still be challenges in reaching consensus on when AGI has truly been achieved. The transition from narrow AI to AGI is likely to be gradual, with systems progressively meeting more criteria over time. Additionally, some aspects (like consciousness or subjective experience) may remain difficult to quantify or verify.

## Affective computing and Emotional AI

On the road to AGI, one of the key areas to emulate is human empathy, with technologies that could detect and respond to human emotions. Affective computing and emotional AI are pivotal fields evolving rapidly to enable machines to recognize, interpret, and respond to human emotions. By bridging the gap between human emotional expression and machine understanding, these technologies are enhancing human-machine interactions across various sectors, including healthcare, education, customer service, and entertainment. Recent significant progress has been made in how AI detects and responds to emotions, using cutting-edge technologies that promise a more empathetic and emotionally responsive AI.

For example, the Japanese company Empath has developed AI that analyzes vocal tones to assess emotional states; it can determine if a user is happy, angry, etc. and the technology is being integrated into various industries, including call centers and customer support, where agents are equipped with real-time emotional feedback from callers, allowing for more empathetic support.

These developments enable AI systems to more accurately detect and respond to human emotions through various modalities, including facial expressions, voice analysis, text sentiment, and physiological signals. Multimodal approaches, combining data from multiple sources, have further enhanced the accuracy and reliability of emotional insights. This integration is rapidly expanding in areas like conversational AI, recommender systems, healthcare platforms, gaming, and educational tools, increasingly incorporating emotion-aware features to provide more personalized and empathetic experiences. In sales and marketing, offerings could be tailored to respond to emotion. Chatbots could adjust their tone based on a user's emotional state, while healthcare applications can detect early signs of mental health issues and offer timely support. Overall, affective computing would prove crucial in areas that most value the human touch, including but not limited to services such as counseling, coaching, and therapy.

However, as previously discussed, these technologies do raise ethical concerns such as data privacy—emotional data is sensitive and must be protected by strict regulations to prevent misuse. There is also risk of manipulation by AI systems that could influence decision-making, e.g., AI that would capitalize on emotional states to influence purchasing and other types of behavior. Also, incorrect emotional interpretation could lead to unhelpful responses in the best-case scenario, but also to actions that could harm users.

Overall, it would be important to reflect on the knock-on effects of increasingly *emotional* humanlike AI.

## What to Expect on the Road to AGI

In the short term some indicators we could expect from hAI are more **natural** interfaces to interact with, for example with voice conversations that are increasingly humanlike; **multimodal** inputs including but not limited to text, voice, images, and video. This could also include extended reality display, glasses, lenses, etc.; better **memory** including but not limited to larger context windows in LLMs; **smarter,** more capable models with higher order reasoning; **agentic**, resulting in more proactive and autonomous systems that are increasingly able to complete tasks and jobs; **invisible** as they are embedded into software and hardware; **architecture-agnostic**, where the transformer is complemented and/or superseded by other hAI technologies; **interfaced**, with brain-machine linking that allows quicker connectivity; and **embodied**, where hAI gains a physical presence, just like Clara.

In the medium term, perhaps one of the most important signs that we are nearing AGI will be the development of cognitive and technical capabilities that extend far beyond current AI systems. AGI will exhibit the ability to generalize across multiple fields, demonstrating true flexibility and adaptability without requiring specific retraining for every task. A hallmark of AGI would be its ability to apply knowledge and skills from one field to entirely different domains. For instance, an AI capable of excelling in medical diagnostics, legal reasoning, and creative writing without specialized programming or retraining would point toward the emergence of general intelligence.

AGI would demonstrate a nuanced comprehension of human emotions, social cues, and complex ethical considerations, something current AI struggles to achieve. This contextual understanding will allow AGI to engage with humans in more intuitive and meaningful ways, reflecting common sense reasoning in decision-making and problem-solving.

Another key indicator of AGI would be its capacity for recursive self-improvement, meaning that it can autonomously enhance its capabilities. This is partly why James Barrat calls AGI our final invention, it would be a creation that reinvents *itself*.

As discussed previously, while cognitive capabilities are essential, AGI would also need to demonstrate emotional intelligence and the ability to engage in human relationships. Current AI systems are transactional, responding to prompts based on pre-programmed algorithms. AGI, on the other hand, will interact with humans in ways that feel genuinely intuitive and empathetic. AGI will possess the ability to engage with humans on a deeper, more intuitive level. It will understand emotional and cultural contexts, making it capable of forming partnerships that resemble human-to-human interactions.

Another significant indicator would be AGI's ability to autonomously navigate ethical dilemmas and make moral judgments. For AGI to be truly effective in human society, it must address issues of fairness, bias, and justice with a level of sophistication that rivals human reasoning. AGI would need to foster genuine emotional connections, understanding human vulnerability, emotions, and relationships with the depth of a human counselor. This emotional intelligence would mark a shift from AI as a tool to AI as a social entity capable of meaningful relationships.

Another key sign of approaching AGI would be its ability to make autonomous decisions and pursue long-term goals without constant human supervision. This autonomy will span various domains, from high-stakes industries to strategic planning on a global scale. AGI would formulate and execute complex, long-term objectives in uncertain and dynamic environments. Whether it's managing a large-scale project or devising strategies for global governance, AGI would demonstrate foresight and strategic thinking that matches, or even exceeds human capabilities. AGI might begin to manage high-stakes environments like finance, healthcare, and even government functions without human intervention. This operational autonomy, especially in fields where failure could have severe consequences, will be a clear indicator of AGI's maturity. AGI would not only serve individual tasks but will actively contribute to global goals such as peace, environmental conservation, and societal well-being. Its decisions will reflect wisdom and compassion, aiming for long-term benefits to humanity and the planet.

The final and most encompassing sign would be AGI's seamless integration into human systems, influencing both physical and digital environments. AGI could operate autonomously across interconnected systems, shaping societal and economic infrastructures with little to no human oversight. AGI's ability to coordinate complex operations—such as managing cities, factories, or even entire countries—without human intervention will be a defining sign of its arrival. AGI might integrate into both physical and digital spaces, from controlling traffic systems to optimizing energy consumption, etc.

All in all, it is useful to think of AGI not as a single moment in time but as a series of interconnected advancements across multiple domains ranging from cognitive breakthroughs and emotional intelligence to autonomous decision-making and societal impact.

## Forces Driving AGI Development

Finally, let's look at some of the forces driving AGI development, to get an intuition for its accelerating pace based on forces such as business demand and technological progress:

| Category | Key Force | Description |
|---|---|---|
| **Technological Drivers** | Computational Advancements | Exponential growth in processing power, memory capacity, and algorithmic efficiency |
| | Machine Learning Progress | Breakthroughs in neural networks, deep learning, and other AI architectures |
| | Data Processing Innovations | Novel techniques for handling and analyzing large-scale datasets |
| **Economic Factors** | Market Incentives | Substantial financial investments from private sector due to potential economic value |
| | Automation Demand | Industries seeking to optimize operations through advanced AI solutions |
| | Competition Dynamics | Global "AI race" among nations and corporations for technological supremacy |
| **Scientific Motivations** | Intellectual Challenge | Researchers driven by the goal of replicating human-level cognition |
| | Interdisciplinary Convergence | Integration of insights from neuroscience, psychology, and computer science |
| | Potential for Scientific Breakthroughs | AGI as a tool for accelerating discoveries in various fields |
| **Societal Influences** | Public Awareness and Interest | Growing cultural fascination with AI and its potential impacts |
| | Ethical and Philosophical Inquiries | Debates on consciousness, intelligence, and the nature of mind |
| | Policy and Regulatory Developments | Government initiatives and frameworks shaping AI research directions |
| **Strategic Considerations** | Military Applications | Defense sector investments in AI for tactical and strategic advantages |
| | Global Problem-Solving Potential | AGI as a means to address complex challenges like climate change and healthcare |
| | Long-term Human Development | Exploration of AI's role in the future of human evolution and space exploration |

*Figure 10. Drivers of AGI development*

The forces driving AGI development are deeply interconnected. What's transformative isn't just the speed of progress, but how these drivers reinforce each other. As businesses invest more, technological innovations accelerate, leading to increased competition, which pushes AGI capabilities even further.

While the original motivation to build thinking machines remains, it's now supercharged by market dynamics. This pursuit represents humanity's quest to automate intelligence and solve complex problems, promising solutions to global challenges while raising profound questions about ethics and societal impact.

Ultimately AGI development reflects humankind's spirit of curiosity and exploration and the centuries-old quest to emulate human intelligence. At the heart of it might be the need to prove that we can conquer yet another technological challenge, this one unlike others: we are using human intelligence to, well, emulate human intelligence. The circularity of this is ironic in a way and also poetic.

# 9
## Dystopia and Utopia
### STAGES OF HUMAN-MACHINE SYNERGY

*Progress is impossible without change, and those who
cannot change their minds cannot change anything.*

*–George Bernard Shaw*

E arlier today my daughter and I were trying
ChatGPT's new advanced voice mode on the
phone app and we had a natural, real-time
conversation with Juniper (one of the preset voices).
We asked "her" to speak in different languages and the
tone was highly realistic, responding naturally to
"humor, sarcasm, interruptions, and more" (per the
documentation). Beyond that, it struck me that it knew
who was talking and addressed each person correctly
and overall, she seemed like a fairly capable
conversationalist. My daughter continued talking to
Juniper for a bit, practicing her Spanish and it struck
me: we are closing the IQ gap where AI assistants
become advanced tutors. The potential applications in
education alone would be nothing short of
transformational.

But to get a balanced view let's explore contrasting
scenarios: AI dystopia vs AI utopia.

## AI dystopia

Imagine a world where the promise of AI has turned dark. Physical stores and human workers have been replaced by tireless machines and algorithms, creating unprecedented economic displacement. An elite few control AI systems that make increasingly automated decisions about healthcare, justice, and social services, decisions that might be efficient but lack human empathy and understanding.

In this scenario, privacy erodes under AI-powered surveillance, while democracy faces new challenges from sophisticated AI-driven manipulation of public opinion. What's particularly concerning is how this affects human value and creativity; artists and knowledge workers find themselves increasingly sidelined by AI systems that can reason, create, and perform any cognitive task more efficiently.

The education system becomes AI-driven, preparing children for a world where human agency is diminished. Above all looms the specter of superintelligent AI, potentially unpredictable and uncontrollable. This isn't just about economic displacement; it's about a fundamental crisis in human purpose and identity as our creations reshape society in ways we no longer fully control.

## AI Utopia

Now imagine a world where AI has become a well-aligned presence that lifts humanity to new heights of prosperity and genuine fulfillment. Streets buzz with autonomous vehicles while passengers engage in discussions about art, philosophy, or their latest creative ventures. Homes are marvels of efficiency, with AI systems that anticipate needs and manage daily routines seamlessly.

The nature of work has fundamentally shifted. Three-day work weeks become the norm, not out of necessity, but for personal growth and societal contribution. People spend their abundant free time pursuing what were once considered luxuries: artistic expression, scientific exploration, or cultivating meaningful relationships. Healthcare has been transformed through AI doctors providing personalized, round-the-clock care, while education becomes a lifelong journey of discovery with AI tutors adapting to each person's unique potential.

Climate change has been effectively addressed through AI-driven innovations in clean energy and resource management. Income inequality has dramatically decreased through universal basic income and near-free access to goods and services. Cities have evolved into green havens, with vertical gardens and clean energy systems integrated into stunning architectural designs.

In research facilities, humans and AI collaborate to unlock universal mysteries, while art galleries showcase an inspiring fusion of human and AI creativity. This isn't a future where humanity has been diminished; it's one where our potential has been magnified. It's a world where being human means exploring, creating, and connecting in ways we once could only dream of, free from the constraints of survival and scarcity.

## Managing Dystopia or Utopia

For Vinod Khosla, a renowned venture capitalist and pioneer in disruptive technologies, AI represents both a utopian and dystopian potential. As a co-founder of Sun Microsystems and the founder of Khosla Ventures, Khosla has a deep understanding of technological advancements and their societal impacts. He views AI as a transformative force that could either greatly benefit or harm society, depending on how it is managed.

In a dystopian future, Khosla warns of AI job loss, economic inequality, social control, and the erosion of human agency and creativity. However, he remains optimistic that with the right policies and regulations, these risks can be mitigated. Khosla believes AI can lead to a utopian world where humans are liberated from mundane tasks, healthcare and education are democratized, and a post-scarcity society emerges, driven by efficiency, sustainability, and human well-being. He emphasizes that while the challenges are real, the potential for AI to create an era of human flourishing outweighs the dystopian risks if humanity navigates its development wisely.

## AI-driven Abundance

If harnessed correctly, AGI and automation could free us from many of today's economic, social, and environmental challenges, as discussed. But the path to this abundant future is probably not a straightforward one.

If healthcare were no longer a privilege but a universally accessible service, everyone could receive the highest quality of care—an era where early detection of diseases and personalized treatment plans extend life expectancy and improve the quality of life. Telemedicine and wearable AI health monitors could eliminate geographical barriers, providing constant health feedback, enabling early interventions, and reshaping healthcare from reactive to preventive.

This revolution would empower not only individual health but also societal well-being. With AI managing our health more efficiently, medical professionals could focus on complex human interactions and novel treatments, allowing healthcare systems to serve more people at lower costs.

## Post-scarcity and Economic Abundance

Part of the transformation could come from the move toward post-scarcity—a world where basic needs such as food, housing, and healthcare are universally met. Automation and AI could manage physical and cognitive tasks, optimizing resource production and distribution so effectively that scarcity, as we know it, becomes a relic of the past.

## Flourishing of Human Potential

With advanced AI managing industries from agriculture to manufacturing, we could witness an unprecedented shift toward equity, sustainability, and quality of life. People could look beyond survival mode, progressively shifting toward higher-order pursuits: creativity, education, and exploration. But this transition will require deep societal shifts—rethinking how we work, earn, and live.

As automation takes over routine and labor-intensive tasks, humans would be free to pursue passions, arts, and intellectual endeavors that make us uniquely human. We could witness a renaissance of human creativity, with AI supporting lifelong learning, enabling individuals to continuously acquire new skills. Art, science, and philosophy could reach new heights as people are liberated to engage fully in intellectual and creative pursuits. But this transition will probably not be without much trial and error, gauging the success or limitations of public policies in guiding innovation, labor relations, societal changes, etc. This will be a profound shift across societies, embraced and repelled at the same time.

## Job Displacement and Economic Instability

AGI and automation will undoubtedly dislocate traditional labor markets. As machines take over cognitive and manual tasks, job displacement could lead to widespread economic instability. We'll need to rethink workforce development, placing a stronger emphasis on human-AI collaboration, retraining, and reskilling. Governments and corporations will need to provide social safety nets, perhaps through policies like Universal Basic Income (UBI), to cushion the impact of these changes.

The psychological toll of job displacement—where many might struggle to find purpose in a post-work world—cannot be underestimated. Society will need new frameworks for meaning, identity, and contribution as AI increasingly takes over traditional human roles.

## Exacerbation of Inequality

As with any technological advancement, there is a risk that the benefits of AGI could be unevenly distributed. Without careful management, AGI could exacerbate existing inequalities, concentrating wealth and power in the hands of a few who control these technologies. Governments, institutions, and civil society must work to ensure that the wealth generated by this abundance is distributed equitably.

## Utopia or Dystopia?

As we envision a future shaped by AI, we must balance the promise of utopia against the very real risks of dystopian outcomes. Could the same technologies that promise universal healthcare, abundance, and freedom also drive us toward social control, surveillance, and loss of autonomy? AI could be used to exacerbate inequalities, control populations, and strip individuals of their privacy. We could see the rise of AI-driven surveillance states, where governments and corporations wield AI as a tool for manipulation, rather than liberation.

Think of some unsettling episodes of *Black Mirror*, the dystopian sci-fi series painting scenarios of pervasive tracking, predicting, and manipulating human behavior with uncanny accuracy. Deepfakes, misinformation, and AI-generated content could erode trust in media and destabilize democracies. In this future, AI serves not as a tool for human flourishing but as an instrument of control and division.

**The Ethical Imperative**

To navigate this era full awareness of hAI development coupled with clear ethical governance ought to become a priority. How we manage the development and implementation of AGI will shape our future—whether we lean toward utopia or dystopia. Governments, technologists, and citizens must actively engage in shaping policies that promote fairness, transparency, and human dignity in the face of rapid AI-driven changes.

## Choosing Our Path

The journey to this new world is not guaranteed to end in utopia or dystopia. It will likely be a continuum—a place where elements of both possibilities coexist, reflecting the choices that we make today in how we develop, deploy, and regulate AGI.

If this transition is managed carefully, AI-driven abundance could be the new normal. Regardless, civilization will require adaptation, thoughtful governance, and the commitment to steer us all toward equity and human flourishing.

## The Four AGI Scenario Wager

Perhaps one of the key questions for decision makers today is: what is the risk of inaction? In other words, is it a waste of resources to actively prepare for an AGI future? Would the opportunity cost of preparing for it outweigh potential benefits? Strategically speaking we can see this as a wager with four scenarios: (1) AGI arrives, and we are prepared, (2) AGI arrives, and we are unprepared, (3) AGI doesn't arrive, but we are prepared, and (4) AGI doesn't arrive, and we didn't prepare.

Clearly the most undesirable scenario is (2) whereas decision makers can be seen as visionary leaders if (1) is realized under their watch. However, along with the potential benefits, all four scenarios carry their own set of risks.

In scenario (1) resource allocation is the main concern. Selling AGI to all relevant stakeholders is not necessarily a straightforward proposition. If you're a public company, the market might react negatively. There are opportunity costs, as talent and resources that could be used elsewhere must be directed towards

AGI prep. However the upside is significant as the organization will be in prime position to harness the benefits of AGI.

Scenario (3) is inconvenient for decision makers: you prepared but nothing happened; you might be left with significant investments for a transformation that never materialized or is playing out much slower than anticipated. It's like planning for a party where the birthday guests never arrive... or arrive a day or two late. While inconvenient, there are still likely many upsides to this approach while overpreparing. Given all evidence on the current trajectory and speed of hAI, it is likely that organizations could still have significant gains that could offset preparation costs, and in a best-case scenario could point towards an enhanced position as an innovative market player.

Scenario (4) is blissful in the sense that nothing significant happens and the organization didn't prepare; the status quo is kept. However, while organizations are spared of significant costs, they are not necessarily leading, and at best might be fast followers from an hAI innovation perspective.

Scenario (2) places organizations in the unenviable position of being caught off guard with no significant organizational awareness, a low hAI skill level and generally a position incompatible with hAI integration—the organization doesn't seem to *get* hAI and once it does it is too late. The company is sent scrambling to react and the ship may be not be able to steer fast enough towards safe harbor.

## The Maximin Approach to AGI Preparedness

The Maximin Principle is a concept introduced by philosopher John Rawls. It is a rule for making decisions under uncertainty. It suggests that one should choose the option that maximizes the minimum possible outcome.

When applying the Maximin Principle to our four AGI scenarios, organizations may follow this approach. First, identify the minimum (worst) outcome for each strategic choice:

| **If we choose not to prepare:** |
| --- |
| Minimum (worst) outcome: AGI arrives and we're unprepared (scenario 2) - potentially catastrophic |
| Best outcome: AGI doesn't arrive and we saved resources (scenario 4) - status quo |
| **If we choose to prepare:** |
| Minimum (worst) outcome: AGI doesn't arrive but we've invested in preparation (scenario 3) - inconvenient but still beneficial |
| Best outcome: AGI arrives and we're ready (scenario 1) - optimal position |

The Maximin approach then tells us to compare these minimum outcomes and choose the strategy with the better minimum. Since scenario 3 (prepared but no AGI) is clearly better than scenario 2 (unprepared when AGI arrives), the Maximin Principle directs organizations to choose preparation.

This isn't just about avoiding disaster, it's about ensuring that even our worst-case scenario still leaves us in a stronger position. By preparing for AGI, we've eliminated the possibility of the truly catastrophic outcome, while building capabilities that benefit the organization regardless of how AGI develops.

# 10

## Shaping the Future

### THRIVING IN THE ERA OF hAI

*The future enters into us, in order to transform itself in us,*
*long before it happens.*

*—Rainer Maria Rilke*

We started this journey by looking at the nature of intelligence, examining its evolution from the unique spark that propelled human progress to the rise of artificial systems capable of mimicking our cognitive abilities. From the early attempts to replicate intelligence in machines, we traced the development of humanlike AI, understanding its transformative impact on industries, decision-making, and creativity. We explored the ethical dilemmas, societal shifts, and associated governance challenges while considering the profound implications for work, identity, and human flourishing. Finally, we reflected on our role in shaping a future where AI amplifies our humanity, ensuring that it serves to enhance, not diminish, what makes us truly human.

## Going forward

Assuming that AGI is realized, regardless of the timeline, the question that I get asked and the question that I often ask myself is:

*What can we do to prepare and make the most of hAI?*

Whether you're leading a business, building a career, or raising children, as we have seen, increasingly powerful humanlike AI offers both opportunities and challenges. Here are some thoughts on how to engage as active participants to help shape our collective future:

**Be Aware**

The first step in any significant transformation is awareness. AGI will not resemble the traditional IT systems we're used to—this is something profoundly different, and it's vital to grasp the nature of human-AI interaction (hAI). Start by deepening your understanding of AI's capabilities and limitations. Become digitally literate, even if you're not a tech expert. Take time to explore what hAI is today and where it's going. The AI landscape is evolving rapidly, so keep your finger on the pulse of AI development by reading, attending webinars, or engaging in online communities focused on AI. Make it part of your routine to stay updated, whether by following leading voices in the field or subscribing to newsletters that track advancements. Knowing where AI is headed allows you to anticipate changes and adjust your course before the world moves too far ahead.

## Experiment and Upskill

Whether you're in business, education, or any creative field, the key to staying relevant is embracing lifelong learning. Upskilling means familiarizing yourself with how to use AI tools to enhance your work but do it in a way that feels like you are playing and experimenting. Follow your curiosity: let it guide you toward applications that resonate with your interests or professional goals. Be prepared to adapt, especially learning to work with hAI as your copilot or digital colleague. Cultivate the ability to learn quickly, unlearn outdated knowledge, and relearn new concepts. The ability to reinvent oneself or one's business model will be one of the most valuable assets in the coming age. Be patient with yourself as you expand your comfort zone and your toolkit.

## Add value with hAI

Integrate hAI into your personal and professional workflows. Build with it, co-create with it, problem-solve with it, and push the boundaries of what can be done. Entrepreneurs can leverage AI to optimize workflows, improve product design, or personalize customer interactions. The key is to stay active, working with hAI as an increasingly capable collaborator, not just a tool. As AI tools become more integrated into our lives, resist the urge to become complacent. Ask questions, experiment with new tools, and push boundaries. Whether it's finding new ways to collaborate with AI on creative projects or exploring entirely new fields, keep pursuing new ways to innovate and grow. Little by little, expand your comfort zone and your toolkit.

## Stay Engaged

AI is not just a technical transformation; it's a societal one. Engage in discussions about AI's implications for the future of work, privacy, ethics, and society. These conversations matter because they shape public policy and influence the way AI systems are designed and implemented. Be vocal about your concerns, your hopes, and your vision for a future where AI serves the public good. By participating in debates and dialogues, you help ensure that AI reflects a diversity of needs and perspectives. Support initiatives that promote ethical AI guidelines and transparent development practices. AI is a powerful tool that will shape the future of our society, and we all have a role in ensuring it's used to improve lives, not exacerbate inequalities. Push for frameworks that ensure fair, safe, and inclusive AI development, helping bridge gaps and foster equity.

## Stay Nimble

Be prepared to adapt as new developments emerge. Seek out new challenges and opportunities to apply AI in innovative ways, resisting the urge to become complacent. Whether it's finding new ways to collaborate with AI on creative projects, or exploring entirely new fields, keep pursuing new ways to innovate and grow.

## Help others

As you learn and expand your capabilities, share your knowledge. The more people understand AI, the more empowered they'll be to use it ethically and effectively. Whether it's through your social circles, community groups, or professional networks, spread awareness about AI's potential and encourage others to explore it thoughtfully. Your guidance could inspire the next wave of innovators.

**Support ethical, safe, inclusive development**

Support initiatives that promote ethical AI guidelines and transparent development practices. AI is a powerful tool that will shape the future of our society, and we all have a role in ensuring it's used to improve lives, not exacerbate inequalities. Push for frameworks that ensure fair, safe, and inclusive AI development, helping bridge gaps and foster equity.

## Philosophical reflections

When I deliver a course, toward the end I like to take a few moments to reflect on what we might value most in a world that has been transformed by AI. In a future where many of our interactions in areas like health, retail, education, banking, and transportation might be with AI agents, participants point out that the human touch will be extra appreciated—knowing that a person has made time for us; knowing that a flesh-and-bone human *cares*. I agree that caring, kindness, and experiencing the uniqueness of human connection would be greatly valued in a world where humanlike AI agents are universally available.

The "human premium" will remain one of the key value propositions that only humans can offer. The *original* human touch, even if there is a more streamlined artificial one available, would be highly appreciated. But then I think—and I confess it does send a chill through me—that given enough time, perhaps over a few generations, this appreciation for the original human touch might also fade away, especially as the younger ones get used to their new AI companions, *digital people*, coexisting with humankind and becoming part of society, especially once affective computing can more fully emulate human emotions.

## From fantasy to reality

I do remain cautiously optimistic about humanity's future, and I do think we can get it right; being fair and inclusive in sharing its benefits, etc. It is a future that must be proactively designed and ethically managed. This promise of AI-driven abundance can be more than a fantasy, it can become our reality.

And speaking of fantasy, today when I watch *Star Wars*, I no longer see C3PO and other humanoid robots as far stretches of the imagination (embodied AGIs). The fact that I catch myself thinking this surely must be a sign, even a faint anecdotal one, that the trajectory to achieve AGI is a plausible one.

# Epilogue
## BEING HUMAN

*The stars, like dust, encircle me*
*In living mists of light;*
*And all of space I seem to see*
*In one vast burst of sight.*
*—Isaac Asimov*

S ome 80 thousand years ago, someone was probably gazing up at the night sky, marveling at a shooting star or the beauty of the Milky Way, having no idea what it meant, what lay beyond the darkness dotted by minuscule points of light. Today, we know a little bit more about our Universe. We've mapped the galaxies, named the stars, and sent probes into interstellar space[2]. We're eager to venture out further, driven by the same curiosity that made our ancestors gaze upward in awe. And perhaps, one day, some version of humankind might go out there, to the very star systems that our earliest ancestors gazed at.

## Being human

Amid the technological wonders we are creating, the trajectory of it all, and the possibilities for humanity, I hope that a version of utopia is possible, that we can

---

[2] As of 2024, the Voyager 1 and Voyager 2 spacecraft, launched in 1977, have crossed the heliopause and entered interstellar space. However, they have not yet reached the theoretical outer edge of the Solar System, which is believed to be the outer boundary of the Oort Cloud.

make it work for humanity (certainly not without trial and error), that we can harness humanlike AI for common good.

And I find myself with more questions than answers.

But one thing is even clearer now: in light of increasingly capable humanlike artificial intelligence, I find stronger cause to be more uniquely, intensely, and authentically... *human*.

# Bibliography

## Chapter 1. Intelligence Built Civilization

Ambrose, S. H. (2001). Paleolithic Technology and Human Evolution. Science, 291(5509), 1748-1753. https://www.science.org/doi/10.1126/science.1059487

Coolidge, F. L., & Wynn, T. (2018). The Rise of Homo sapiens: The Evolution of Modern Thinking. Oxford University Press. https://www.researchgate.net/publication/259862100_The_rise_of_ Homo_sapiens_the_evolution_of_modern_thinking_- _By_Frederick_L_Coolidge_Thomas_Wynn

d'Errico, F., & Stringer, C. B. (2011). Evolution, revolution or saltation scenario for the emergence of modern cultures? Philosophical Transactions of the Royal Society B: Biological Sciences, 366(1567), 1060-1069. https://www.ncbi.nlm.nih.gov/pmc/articles/PMC3049097/

Gardner, H. (2011). Frames of Mind: The Theory of Multiple Intelligences. Basic Books.

Gottfredson, L. S. (1997). Mainstream science on intelligence: An editorial with 52 signatories, history, and bibliography. Intelligence, 24(1), 13-23. https://www1.udel.edu/educ/gottfredson/reprints/1997mainstream.p df

Harari, Y. N. (2015). Sapiens: A Brief History of Humankind. Harper.

McBrearty, S., & Brooks, A. S. (2000). The revolution that wasn't: a new interpretation of the origin of modern human behavior. Journal of Human Evolution, 39(5), 453-563. https://www.sciencedirect.com/science/article/abs/pii/S0047248400 904354

Mithen, S. (1996). The Prehistory of the Mind: The Cognitive Origins of Art, Religion and Science. Thames and Hudson.

Neubauer, S., Hublin, J. J., & Gunz, P. (2018). The evolution of modern human brain shape. Science Advances, 4(1), eaao5961. https://www.science.org/doi/10.1126/sciadv.aao5961

Piaget, J. (1952). The Origins of Intelligence in Children. International Universities Press.

Pinker, S. (2010). The Language Instinct: How the Mind Creates Language. William Morrow Paperbacks.

Stringer, C. (2016). The origin and evolution of Homo sapiens. Philosophical Transactions of the Royal Society B: Biological Sciences, 371(1698), 20150237. https://www.ncbi.nlm.nih.gov/pmc/articles/PMC4920294/

Tattersall, I. (2012). Masters of the Planet: The Search for Our Human Origins. Palgrave Macmillan.

Tomasello, M. (2014). A Natural History of Human Thinking. Harvard University Press.

Vygotsky, L. S. (1986). Thought and Language. MIT Press.

Wechsler, D. (1958). The Measurement and Appraisal of Adult Intelligence. Williams & Wilkins.

Winegard, B., Winegard, B., & Boutwell, B. (2017). Human Biological and Psychological Diversity. Evolutionary Psychological Science, 3, 159-180. https://link.springer.com/article/10.1007/s40806-016-0081-5Txt

## Chapter 2. Thinking Machines

Babbage, C. (1864). Passages from the Life of a Philosopher. Longman, Green, Longman, Roberts, & Green. https://www.gutenberg.org/files/57532/57532-h/57532-h.htm

Buchanan, B. G. (2005). A (Very) Brief History of Artificial Intelligence. AI Magazine, 26(4), 53-60. https://ojs.aaai.org/aimagazine/index.php/aimagazine/article/view/1848

Goodfellow, I., Bengio, Y., & Courville, A. (2016). Deep Learning. MIT Press. https://www.deeplearningbook.org/

LeCun, Y., Bengio, Y., & Hinton, G. (2015). Deep learning. Nature, 521(7553), 436-444. https://www.nature.com/articles/nature14539

Legg, S., & Hutter, M. (2007). Universal Intelligence: A Definition of Machine Intelligence. Minds and Machines, 17(4), 391-444. https://arxiv.org/abs/0712.3329

McCarthy, J., Minsky, M. L., Rochester, N., & Shannon, C. E. (2006). A Proposal for the Dartmouth Summer Research Project on Artificial Intelligence, August 31, 1955. AI Magazine, 27(4), 12-14. https://doi.org/10.1609/aimag.v27i4.1904

Minsky, M. (1986). The Society of Mind. Simon and Schuster.

Nilsson, N. J. (2009). The Quest for Artificial Intelligence: A History of Ideas and Achievements. Cambridge University Press. https://ai.stanford.edu/~nilsson/QAI/qai.pdf

Russell, S., & Norvig, P. (2020). Artificial Intelligence: A Modern Approach (4th ed.). Pearson.

Searle, J. R. (1980). Minds, brains, and programs. Behavioral and Brain Sciences, 3(3), 417-424. https://doi.org/10.1017/S0140525X00005756

Silver, D., Hubert, T., Schrittwieser, J., Antonoglou, I., Lai, M., Guez, A., ... & Hassabis, D. (2018). A general reinforcement learning algorithm that masters chess, shogi, and Go through self-play. Science, 362(6419), 1140-1144. https://www.science.org/doi/10.1126/science.aar6404

Turing, A. M. (1950). Computing Machinery and Intelligence. Mind, 59(236), 433-460. https://academic.oup.com/mind/article/LIX/236/433/986238

**Chapter 3. Artificial Intelligence**

Amodei, D., Hernandez, D., Sastry, G., Clark, J., Brockman, G., & Sutskever, I. (2018). AI and Compute. OpenAI. https://openai.com/research/ai-and-compute

Bengio, Y., Lecun, Y., & Hinton, G. (2021). Deep Learning for AI. Communications of the ACM, 64(7), 58-65. https://doi.org/10.1145/3448250

Geirhos, R., Jacobsen, J. H., Michaelis, C., Zemel, R., Brendel, W., Bethge, M., & Wichmann, F. A. (2020). Shortcut Learning in Deep Neural Networks. Nature Machine Intelligence, 2(11), 665-673. https://www.nature.com/articles/s42256-020-00257-z

Immordino-Yang, M. H., & Damasio, A. (2007). We feel, therefore we learn: The relevance of affective and social neuroscience to education. Mind, Brain, and Education, 1(1), 3-10. https://onlinelibrary.wiley.com/doi/abs/10.1111/j.1751-228X.2007.00004.x

Mar, R. A. (2011). The neural bases of social cognition and story comprehension. Annual Review of Psychology, 62, 103-134. https://www.annualreviews.org/doi/abs/10.1146/annurev-psych-120709-145406

Marcus, G. (2018). Deep Learning: A Critical Appraisal. arXiv preprint arXiv:1801.00631. https://arxiv.org/abs/1801.00631

**Chapter 4. Growing a Brain**

Brown, T. B., Mann, B., Ryder, N., Subbiah, M., Kaplan, J., Dhariwal, P., ... & Amodei, D. (2020). Language Models are Few-Shot Learners. arXiv preprint arXiv:2005.14165. https://arxiv.org/abs/2005.14165

Devlin, J., Chang, M. W., Lee, K., & Toutanova, K. (2018). BERT: Pre-training of Deep Bidirectional Transformers for Language Understanding. arXiv preprint arXiv:1810.04805. https://arxiv.org/abs/1810.04805

Radford, A., Wu, J., Child, R., Luan, D., Amodei, D., & Sutskever, I. (2019). Language Models are Unsupervised Multitask Learners. OpenAI Blog, 1(8), 9. https://cdn.openai.com/better-language-models/language_models_are_unsupervised_multitask_learners.pdf

Vaswani, A., Shazeer, N., Parmar, N., Uszkoreit, J., Jones, L., Gomez, A. N., ... & Polosukhin, I. (2017). Attention is All You Need. In Advances in Neural Information Processing Systems (pp. 5998-6008). https://papers.nips.cc/paper/2017/file/3f5ee243547dee91fbd053c1c4a845aa-Paper.pdf

Wang, A., Singh, A., Michael, J., Hill, F., Levy, O., & Bowman, S. R. (2018). GLUE: A Multi-Task Benchmark and Analysis Platform for Natural Language Understanding. arXiv preprint arXiv:1804.07461. https://arxiv.org/abs/1804.07461

Wolf, T., Debut, L., Sanh, V., Chaumond, J., Delangue, C., Moi, A., ... & Rush, A. M. (2020). Transformers: State-of-the-Art Natural Language Processing. In Proceedings of the 2020 Conference on Empirical Methods in Natural Language Processing: System Demonstrations (pp. 38-45). https://www.aclweb.org/anthology/2020.emnlp-demos.6/

## Chapter 5. Capabilities and Use Cases

Accenture. (2023). Technology Vision 2023: When Atoms Meet Bits. https://www.accenture.com/content/dam/accenture/final/accenture-com/document/Accenture-Technology-Vision-2023-Full-Report.pdf

Artificial Intelligence Index Report 2023. (2023). Stanford University Human-Centered AI Institute. https://aiindex.stanford.edu/report/

Gartner. (2023). Gartner Top 10 Strategic Technology Trends for 2024. https://www.gartner.com/en/articles/gartner-top-10-strategic-technology-trends-for-2024

IDC. (2023). Worldwide Artificial Intelligence Spending Guide. https://www.idc.com/getdoc.jsp?containerId=IDC_P33198

IBM. (2023). Global AI Adoption Index 2023. https://filecache.mediaroom.com/mr5mr_ibmspgi/179414/download/IBM%20Global%20AI%20Adoption%20Index%20Report%20Dec.%202023.pdf

McKinsey & Company. (2024). "The State of AI in Early 2024: Gen AI Adoption Spikes."

https://www.mckinsey.com/~/media/mckinsey/business%20function
s/quantumblack/our%20insights/the%20state%20of%20ai/2024/the
-state-of-ai-in-early-2024-final.pdf

World Economic Forum. (2023). The Future of Jobs Report 2023:
AI and the New Economy.
https://www3.weforum.org/docs/WEF_Future_of_Jobs_2023.pdf

## Chapter 6. Risks and Challenges

Acemoglu, D. (2021). Harms of AI. National Bureau of Economic
Research. https://www.nber.org/papers/w29247

Amodei, D., Olah, C., Steinhardt, J., Christiano, P., Schulman, J., &
Mané, D. (2016). Concrete Problems in AI Safety. arXiv preprint
arXiv:1606.06565. https://arxiv.org/abs/1606.06565

Bostrom, N. (2014). Superintelligence: Paths, Dangers, Strategies.
Oxford University Press.

Dafoe, A. (2018). AI Governance: A Research Agenda.
Governance of AI Program, Future of Humanity Institute, University
of Oxford. https://www.fhi.ox.ac.uk/wp-content/uploads/GovAI-
Agenda.pdf

European Commission. (2021). Proposal for a Regulation laying
down harmonised rules on artificial intelligence. https://digital-
strategy.ec.europa.eu/en/library/proposal-regulation-laying-down-
harmonised-rules-artificial-intelligence

Floridi, L., & Cowls, J. (2019). A Unified Framework of Five
Principles for AI in Society. Harvard Data Science Review, 1(1).
https://hdsr.mitpress.mit.edu/pub/l0jsh9d1

Schneier, B. (2021). The Coming AI Hackers. Belfer Center for
Science and International Affairs, Harvard Kennedy School.
https://www.belfercenter.org/publication/coming-ai-hackers

## Chapter 7. Five Transformation Scenarios

Brynjolfsson, E., & McAfee, A. (2014). The Second Machine Age:
Work, Progress, and Prosperity in a Time of Brilliant Technologies.
W. W. Norton & Company.
https://wwnorton.com/books/9780393350647

Chui, M., et al. (2022). AI Adoption Advances, but Foundational
Barriers Remain. McKinsey & Company.
https://www.mckinsey.com/capabilities/mckinsey-digital/our-
insights/the-state-of-ai-in-2022-and-a-half-decade-in-review

Rahwan, I., et al. (2019). Machine Behaviour. Nature.
https://www.nature.com/articles/s41586-019-1138-y

Goodman, B., & Flaxman, S. (2017). European Union Regulations on Algorithmic Decision-Making and a "Right to Explanation". AI Magazine. https://ojs.aaai.org/index.php/aimagazine/article/view/2741

Future of Life Institute. (2023). AI Policy – Global AI Policy. Future of Life Institute. https://futureoflife.org/ai-policy/

## Chapter 8. The Road to AGI

Barrat, J., 2013. Our Final Invention: Artificial Intelligence and the End of the Human Era. New York: Thomas Dunne Books.

Bubeck, S., et al. (2023). Sparks of Artificial General Intelligence: Early Experiments with GPT-4. arXiv preprint arXiv:2303.12712. https://arxiv.org/abs/2303.12712

Grace, K., et al. (2018). When Will AI Exceed Human Performance? Evidence from AI Experts. Journal of Artificial Intelligence Research, 62, 729-754. https://jair.org/index.php/jair/article/view/11222

Hassabis, D., Kumaran, D., Summerfield, C., & Botvinick, M. (2017). Neuroscience-Inspired Artificial Intelligence. Neuron, 95(2), 245-258. https://www.cell.com/neuron/fulltext/S0896-6273(17)30509-3

Ishiguro, H., & Nishio, S. (2007). Building Artificial Humans: A Study on Humanoid Robotics. Science Robotics. https://www.researchgate.net/publication/5993242_Building_artificial_humans_to_understand_humans

Lake, B. M., Ullman, T. D., Tenenbaum, J. B., & Gershman, S. J. (2017). Building Machines That Learn and Think Like People. Behavioral and Brain Sciences, 40, e253. https://doi.org/10.1017/S0140525X16001837

McStay, A. (2020). Emotional AI: The Rise of Empathic Media. SAGE Publications. https://uk.sagepub.com/en-gb/eur/emotional-ai/book251642

Müller, V. C., & Bostrom, N. (2016). Future Progress in Artificial Intelligence: A Survey of Expert Opinion. In V. C. Müller (Ed.), Fundamental Issues of Artificial Intelligence (pp. 555-572). Springer.

Musk E, Neuralink An Integrated Brain-Machine Interface Platform With Thousands of Channels J Med Internet Res 2019;21(10):e16194 https://doi.org/10.2196/16194

Russell, S., & Norvig, P. (2020). Artificial Intelligence: A Modern Approach. Pearson. http://aima.cs.berkeley.edu

Silver, D., et al. (2018). A General Reinforcement Learning Algorithm that Masters Chess, Shogi, and Go through Self-play. Science, 362(6419), 1140-1144. https://www.science.org/doi/10.1126/science.aar6404

## Chapter 9. Dystopia and Utopia

Acemoglu, D., & Restrepo, P. (2019). Automation and New Tasks: How Technology Displaces and Reinstates Labor. Journal of Economic Perspectives, 33(2), 3-30. https://www.aeaweb.org/articles?id=10.1257/jep.33.2.3

Floridi, L. (2019). The Ethics of Artificial Intelligence. In The Oxford Handbook of Ethics of AI. Oxford University Press. https://www.oxfordhandbooks.com/view/10.1093/oxfordhb/9780190 067397.001.0001/oxfordhb-9780190067397-e-1

Ford, M. (2015). Rise of the Robots: Technology and the Threat of a Jobless Future. Basic Books.

Gabriel, I. (2020). Artificial Intelligence, Values, and Alignment. Minds and Machines, 30, 411-437. https://link.springer.com/article/10.1007/s11023-020-09539-2

Harari, Y. N. (2016). Homo Deus: A Brief History of Tomorrow. Harper.

Khosla, V. (2024). AI: Dystopia or Utopia? https://www.khoslaventures.com/ai-dystopia-or-utopia/

Makridakis, S. (2017). The Forthcoming Artificial Intelligence (AI) Revolution: Its Impact on Society and Firms. Futures, 90, 46-60. https://www.sciencedirect.com/science/article/pii/S0016328717300 046

Russell, S. (2019). Human Compatible: Artificial Intelligence and the Problem of Control. Viking.

Topol, E. J. (2019). Deep Medicine: How Artificial Intelligence Can Make Healthcare Human Again. Basic Books.

Van Est, R., & Gerritsen, J. (2017). Human Rights in the Robot Age: Challenges Arising from the Use of Robotics, Artificial Intelligence, and Virtual and Augmented Reality. Rathenau Instituut. https://www.rathenau.nl/en/digital-society/human-rights-robot-age

## Chapter 10. Shaping the Future

Chalmers, D. J. (2010). The Singularity: A Philosophical Analysis. Journal of Consciousness Studies, 17(9-10), 7-65. https://consc.net/papers/singularity.pdf

Domingos, P. (2015). The Master Algorithm: How the Quest for the Ultimate Learning Machine Will Remake Our World. Basic Books.

Harari, Y. N. (2018). 21 Lessons for the 21st Century. Spiegel & Grau.

Kaplan, J. (2016). Artificial Intelligence: What Everyone Needs to Know. Oxford University Press.

Markoff, J. (2015). Machines of Loving Grace: The Quest for Common Ground Between Humans and Robots. Ecco.

Asimov, I. (1950). I, Robot. Gnome Press.

Kurzweil, R. (2005). The Singularity Is Near: When Humans Transcend Biology. Viking.

Sagan, C. (1994). Pale Blue Dot: A Vision of the Human Future in Space. Random House.

Schneider, S. (2019). Artificial You: AI and the Future of Your Mind. Princeton University Press.

Tegmark, M. (2017). Life 3.0: Being Human in the Age of Artificial Intelligence. Knopf.

Vinge, V. (1993). The Coming Technological Singularity: How to Survive in the Post-Human Era. NASA. Lewis Research Center, Vision 21: Interdisciplinary Science and Engineering in the Era of Cyberspace. https://ntrs.nasa.gov/citations/19940022855

# Table of Figures

# About the Author

Victor del Rosal is Chief AI Officer at fiveinnolabs. He has worked as Director of Strategy and Business Development at CloudStrong, Irish cloud services provider, and as Head of Business Analysis for High Tech & Telecom at the Tata Consultancy Services (TCS) Supply Center of Excellence.

Victor is author of the book Disruption: *Emerging Technologies and the Future of Work*, ranked #12 on BookAuthority's Best Technology Trends Books of all time.

He is lecturer of MSc in AI for Business and other Masters programs at National College of Ireland and corporate trainer on generative AI for the UCD Professional Academy (Dublin, Ireland).

# Additional resources

To access the resources mentioned in the book please go to www.humanlikebook.com

Printed in Great Britain
by Amazon

51081511R00098

# HUMANLIKE
## The AI Transformation

Victor del Rosal

fiveinnolabs
Dublin

Published by fiveinnolabs, Republic of Ireland

Sold by: Amazon

ISBN-13: 979-8346218135

*To the dreamers and the doers...*